The Professional Teaching Assistant

Becoming a Primary Higher Level Teaching Assistant

 Richard Rose

Acknowledgements

The author is indebted to colleagues within the School of Education at University College Northampton whose work and ideas have informed this book. He is also grateful to the many teaching assistants who have participated on courses provided through the School of Education and to their schools for supporting both the students and himself. He would also particularly like to say thank you to Sue Bryant, Paul Bramble and Liz Allison whose administrative support makes his task so much easier.

Every effort has been made to trace copyright holders and to obtain their permission for the use of copyright material. The author and publisher will gladly receive any information enabling them to rectify any error or omission in subsequent editions.

First published in 2005 by Learning Matters Ltd.

British Library Cataloguing in Publication Data
A CIP record for this book is available from the British Library.

ISBN 1 84445 025 2

Project Management by Deer Park Productions
Cover design by Code 5 Design Associates Ltd
Typeset by Pantek Arts Ltd, Maidstone, Kent
Printed and bound in Great Britain by Bell & Bain Ltd, Glasgow

Learning Matters Ltd
33 Southernhay East
EXETER EX1 1NX
Tel: 01392 215560
info@learningmatters.co.uk
www.learningmatters.co.uk

Contents

Dedication

This book is dedicated to the memory of my good colleague Bob Walker whose inspiration and commitment to the cause of high quality professional development for teaching assistants has made an immeasurable contribution to the lives of so many colleagues over many years.

Introduction

HOW TO USE THIS BOOK

This book, along with the others in The Professional Teaching Assistant series has been designed not only to assist you in achieving HLTA status, but also to encourage you to reflect upon and learn about the requirements of working in today's classrooms. Working in schools today is a rewarding, though often challenging, experience. The provision of high quality learning experiences to all pupils in a class makes demands upon teachers and teaching assistants with regards to assessment, planning, classroom management and the development of teamwork. The role of the professional teaching assistant has gradually emerged over the past 30 years as a critical one in providing essential support to teachers and enabling all pupils to gain from a positive learning experience. Thomas, writing in 1992, suggests that over a ten year period (1980–90) many adults appeared in classrooms to work alongside teachers as a result of changes in schools which included a recognition of the need to address a wider range of special educational needs in classrooms, and an acknowledgement of the critical role which parents and other adults could play in supporting children's learning. He further suggests that the arrival of more adults in the classroom has required us to reconsider the roles played by teachers and others, including teaching assistants, and to develop more effective ways of creating classroom teams. The recognition of the role of Higher Level Teaching Assistants may be interpreted as an important step in ensuring that we develop classroom teams in a way which is conducive to the effective learning of all pupils.

This book is written in recognition of the fact that the important role played by teaching assistants in our schools and colleges is finally being acknowledged, and that increasing numbers of teaching assistants are seeking further training, qualifications and status within their schools. While the book has the primary objective of supporting teaching assistants as they move towards HLTA status, it is written with a belief that a simplistic approach to passing assessment without contemplating the major issues which influence teaching and learning in our schools, would be doing a disservice to the professional approach adopted by many teaching assistants working in today's classrooms. Our experience of working on courses for teaching assistants over several years has led us to believe that the majority of these colleagues wish to know more about how the pupils with whom they work learn and about how they can become ever more proficient in supporting them. Some of the teaching assistants who progress to HLTA status will go on to train as teachers through one of the many routes now available to them. Others will be satisfied to have had their professionalism recognised through the assessment process. Within this book we have endeavoured to recognise the major professional contribution which teaching assistants make to schools and colleges and to provide a text which we hope will be of value to our professional colleagues whichever route they choose to pursue.

This book begins with the premise that its readers have made a commitment to achieving the highest standards in providing classroom support for all pupils. It sets out not only to assist the reader in gaining the standards for HLTA, but also to provide opportunities for reflection upon how pupils learn and how they may best be supported in that process. Each chapter introduces a critical issue, which has an impact upon the education of all pupils. While a book of this nature can do little more than raise awareness of these issues, through a series of practical tasks and case studies it endeavours to assist the reader in contemplating and analysing those factors which may influence the success or failure of learners in a typical classroom.

It is anticipated that those who read this book are likely to have embarked upon a pathway which they hope will lead them to gain HLTA status. With this in mind, the book has been written to a set format which aims to assist the reader in gaining some understanding of issues, to encourage them to consider these in respect of specific examples and to undertake a series of tasks which will develop their own thinking in respect of these issues.

Each chapter has a brief introduction, which is followed by an outline of the HLTA standards to be considered within the chapter. Inevitably, some of the standards will be addressed in more than one chapter, while others are very focused and may only be considered at a specific point in the book. Early in each chapter you will find a box which outlines what you should have learned once you have read the chapter and completed the tasks within it.

The case studies have all been drawn from the school experiences of colleagues and students with whom we have worked over many years. They are presented as a means of illustrating the principles discussed in the chapter. You may relate these to your own experiences and should always try to reflect upon them in a way that enables you to consider how you would deal with situations in your own school.

The practical tasks provided are designed to encourage you to gather evidence of your own, or your school's, response to a range of situations related to the HLTA standards. In some instances, you may choose to use the evidence gathered from undertaking these tasks as a contribution towards the assessment process. For some of the tasks you will need the co-operation of colleagues or others within your school. It is hoped that by participating in these tasks you may be enabled to engage in a professional dialogue which informs your own thinking and possibly that of others.

At the end of each chapter you will find a summary of key points which indicates some of the most important principles discussed and which you may wish to consider in the light of your own practice and that of others within your school.

This book does draw upon research and refers to a number of other key texts but does so without wishing to overburden you with the task of needing to hunt for additional information unless you wish to do so. The references are listed at the end of each chapter and indicate further reading which you may wish to pursue as you continue your path towards attaining HLTA status.

References

Thomas, G (1992) *Effective classroom teamwork: support or intrusion?* London: Routledge.

1. An introduction to the HLTA Standards
by Ken Bland

This book has been written to help you prepare for the new status of the Higher Level Teaching Assistant (HLTA). In the publication *Time for Standards*, the government set out its plans for the reform of the school workforce. This reform recognised that support staff can, and do, make an increasingly critical contribution to all aspects of the successful operation of schools. At the same time there was an important acknowledgement that, with training and support, many teaching assistants can operate at a higher level than may have been recognised in the past.

The HLTA Standards were published in September 2003 (TTA 2004) and identified the skills and understanding you will need to demonstrate in order to be awarded the status of HLTA. Many teaching assistants, when they first look at these standards, suggest that they already meet many, if not all, of them. You will find that when we look at the standards in detail that this is often the case but that some standards may be more problematic to demonstrate than others. This may be due to the specific situation in which you have been working or to a lack of training with regard to certain elements of the standards. However, the key point to understand is that the status of HLTA is awarded by the Teacher Training Agency (TTA) via a number of Approved Training Providers and that you will need to provide evidence to them that you can meet all of the standards as detailed. The main focus of this chapter is to help you to become familiar with the standards and to help you prepare for this assessment.

Assessment of HLTA status

There are a number of underlying principles informing the assessment of HLTA which can be identified. There needs to be:

- school support for the candidate;
- proficiency in literacy and numeracy (see standard 2.6, pages 11–12);
- assessment that is manageable, rigorous and fit for the purpose;
- assessment that takes no more time than is necessary to demonstrate competence;
- assessment that is based on work that occurs during the normal course of duties;
- responsibility on the part of the candidate to record evidence in support of the assessment.

The first of these principles is important for anyone contemplating going forward for assessment. The support of the school is essential if you are to be able to gather all of the evidence which you require in order to demonstrate that you meet the required standards. Your head teacher will have to agree to your application to go on a HLTA route. It is also helpful to discuss this procedure with your immediate working colleagues as you will be asking for their support at various stages of the process. It is equally essential that at that stage you have a literacy or numeracy qualification at NVQ Level 2 or its equivalent, as you will not be able to proceed successfully without this crucial evidence. Details of what constitutes these levels are available from the TTA website **www.hlta.gov.uk**. The aim of the HLTA programme is that the assessment process should be linked to your normal workload. In other words, you should be in a position to use evidence from your daily working practice in order to support the assessment process. This aim, while laudable, has not, in most cases, been realised and the majority of candidates have undertaken a large amount of additional work in order to ensure that they gain sufficient evidence to satisfy the assessors.

Routes to achieving HLTA status

Currently there are two routes to achieving HLTA status.

1. The assessment only route: this is a three-day route spread over a term and is for more experienced teaching assistants who feel that they already meet the standards.
2. The training route: this route is for teaching assistants who need training in certain standards before they apply for HLTA status.

An early priority must be for you to decide which is the best route for you. This will depend on your current level of expertise and training and your personal confidence in relation to the HLTA standards. This is where having the support of colleagues in school may be particularly helpful as it will give you an opportunity to discuss how both you and they feel about your current experience and expertise.

- If you have limited experience of working in schools as a teaching assistant, and have undertaken very limited training, then you will need to explore how you can extend your knowledge and experience and then apply to go on an HLTA route in the future.
- If you feel that you need further training in order to meet the standards, for example in the areas of SEN or ICT, then the training route is likely to be the most appropriate for you. This route is spread usually over two terms and consists of up to 20 days face-to-face training with experienced providers, 20 days work in schools, and 10 days of computer-based e-learning.
- If you feel that you have considerable knowledge, experience and skills related to the HLTA standards you should apply to go on the assessment only route. However, we would advise that, before making this decision, you examine the HLTA standards carefully to ensure that you are familiar with them, and can provide clear evidence of your ability to meet them in assessment. The task at the end of this chapter is designed to enable you to do this.

A possible third route to HLTA status is for those students who are taking a Foundation Degree or similar degree course. The increase in opportunities to undertake Foundation Degrees has, in many instances, been welcomed by teaching assistants as enabling them to further their own professional knowledge and skills. You will still need to apply for a place on the HLTA via your local LEA and undertake the assessment only route.

There are a number of stages for you to go through and some teaching assistants reading this book will already be on an HLTA programme, while others will be considering applying. The six stages for the three-day assessment route are:

● candidate information;

● two-day briefing;

● assessment tasks;

● one-day briefing and review;

● school visit;

● decision communicated.

PRACTICAL TASK

Consider the position of the following teaching assistants who are considering being assessed for the HLTA. Which of the three assessment routes would you recommend to them and why?

Susan is a teaching assistant currently working within the Foundation Stage. She is currently working towards a Foundation Degree for Teaching Assistants and hopes to achieve Qualified Teacher Status after she is awarded an honours degree. There are two reception classes in the Foundation Stage in her school and Susan plans and delivers sessions on numeracy and creative developments. Susan works closely with the reception teacher. Susan wants to achieve HLTA status as a way of getting onto an employment-based route into teaching.

John is a teaching assistant who has worked in the school for one year and has an excellent awareness of autism spectrum disorders. He works with a year 5 child who has a diagnosis of autistic spectrum disorder and now would like to expand his opportunities to work across the school with other groups of children.

Angela has undertaken a number of courses for teaching assistants at her local university and worked as a Specialist Teaching Assistant for six years. She works with individual pupils, groups and a whole class for dance. She has experience of teaching dance to children and adults at her local community centre.

It is possible to suggest that in the examples provided, John should do the training route, Angela an assessment course and Susan needs to opt for the assessment only route as she is undertaking a Foundation Degree. However, much will depend upon the individual circumstances of the interested teaching assistants as well as factors such as the support of the school in providing opportunities for gaining experience and the confidence with which they each approach the task. These are important factors which you will need to consider when committing yourself to this process. Whichever route is most relevant to you, you will have to undertake the same assessment procedures as all the candidates on the other routes.

Motivation

It is essential that all teaching assistants who approach the route towards gaining HLTA status consider those factors which motivate them to want to proceed. There are many reasons why you may wish to undertake this pathway. Most experienced teaching assistants like Susan and Angela would identify that their jobs have changed compared with when they started. Susan is completing a Foundation Degree in Teaching and Learning and is using the HLTA status as a stepping stone to her ultimate professional goal of becoming a teacher. She has already identified an ambitious pathway which will ultimately lead her to further qualifications in order to join the teaching profession. Angela and John have not, at present, identified the HLTA as leading to a career move. Indeed, they both see the enhanced status of HLTA as their ultimate work-related goal. This, for many professional colleagues will be sufficient in itself as a motivating factor in undertaking the HLTA pathway. The HLTA is not intended as a stepping stone towards gaining a teaching qualification, though some colleagues may find that it is a useful starting point which can be used towards attaining a place on further training courses which may lead to this goal. Whatever your motivation for embarking on the HLTA, you are beginning a process which will lead to a recognition of your professionalism across educational institutions of your skills, knowledge and understanding.

Understanding the HLTA Standards

The HLTA Standards have been designed to assess your skills, knowledge and understanding as a professional and are divided into three sections:

1. Professional values and practice: 1.1 – 1.6;
2. Knowledge and understanding: 2.1 – 2.9;
3. Teaching and learning activities; these are further subdivided into:
   a) Planning and expectations: 3.1.1 – 3.1.4
   b) Monitoring and assessment: 3.2.1 – 3.2.4
   c) Teaching and learning activities: 3.3.1 – 3.3.8.

You will be aware of these standards if you have begun the application process. It is likely that, on viewing these, you may feel that some are fairly straightforward while others are more complex. It is probable that some standards will require some clarification. For example standard 2.7 is: *They are aware of the statutory frameworks relevant to their role*. With this standard there is a need to specify the extent of the knowledge and understanding expected of teaching assistants working at an HLTA level. It is important to specify what is expected of their role and how this expectation will change from, for example, a teaching assistant working in a 6th form college to one working in a nursery school. It is quite probable that you may be more familiar with some of the statutory requirements which relate directly to your current role. For example, if you are working as a teaching assistant supporting pupils with special educational needs, you may well feel quite conversant with the *Special Educational Needs Code of Practice* (2001). However, you may be less familiar with other statutory requirements. The important expression in standard 2.7 relates to *frameworks relevant to their role.* You would not be expected to know every piece of educational legislation but assessors will expect that you can demonstrate an understanding of those which have a direct bearing upon your professional performance.

In the publication *Guidance to the Standards* (TTA 2004) it was noted that:

> *Support staff meeting this standard will be able to demonstrate they are aware of the legal framework that underpins teaching and learning, and broader support and protection for both pupils and adults. Whilst it is not necessary for them to have a detailed knowledge of the whole legal framework they will be aware of their statutory responsibilities and where to gain information, support and assistance when they need it.*
>
> (TTA 2005, p19)

There are, of course, policies and statutes which relate to critical elements such as child protection, of which all professionals working in schools need to have a good working knowledge.

Some standards contain a number of composite statements, for example standard 1.1:

> *They have high expectations of all pupils; respect their social, cultural, linguistic, religious and ethnic backgrounds; and are committed to raising their educational achievement.*

Perhaps you work in a situation where there are few, or even no, children for whom English is an additional language and that there is little cultural diversity within your school. This would not be a reason for being unaware of your responsibilities or for not demonstrating your ability to meet this particular standard. It is quite possible that in the future the nature of your school population may change or that having gained your HLTA status you move to a different school with a more diverse population. It is therefore important that you demonstrate that you can meet this standard in full.

Other standards may be specific to your working situation in other ways. For example, standard 2.2 states that:

> *They are familiar with the school curriculum, the age-related expectations of pupils, the main teaching methods and the testing/examination frameworks in the subjects and age ranges in which they are involved.*

If you are working in a junior school it is to be expected that you are familiar with the requirements of the National Curriculum for pupils working in Key Stage 2. However, it would be reasonable to expect you to have some understanding of the requirements and content from the National Curriculum at both Key Stages 1 and 3 as there may be pupils in your school who, either because of special educational needs or through being gifted or talented, may be working outside of the Programmes of Study for their chronological age. In some instances, in your role as a teaching assistant, you may be supporting pupils in a specific area of the curriculum such as literacy or numeracy and have little input into other subject based lessons. You will, however, be expected to demonstrate an understanding of broader curriculum requirements in respect of the age range with which you are working.

Familiarity with the standards is essential if you are to succeed in providing sufficient evidence to go through the assessment process. You should make full use of the *Guidance to the Standards* document, which will clarify how these are interpreted and provide some useful exemplars. It is equally important that you seek the advice of experienced colleagues in your school who may be able to provide clarification with regard to school policies and point you in the direction of useful information.

As the HLTA standards are demanding, it would be surprising if you did not find that you needed to improve your work in relation to some of these. This book is intended to provide a broad overview which will assist you in attaining the standards but it cannot act as a substitute for your own efforts in gaining information through your school and by engaging in professional conversation with your colleagues. Clearly, if you are undertaking training related to the HLTA you should receive guidance and support from your tutors. However, as stated in the assessment principles, it is anticipated that you will keep your own detailed records to support the assessment process.

PRACTICAL TASK

Self-review

The remaining chapters in this book are designed to assist you in gaining sufficient understanding of the important issues that will enable you to complete assessment. Before proceeding to these, you should complete this task which will help you to review where you are currently positioned in your ability to provide the necessary evidence to complete the assessment. Use the charts provided to undertake a personal review of how you stand in relation to the required standards for HLTA. It is not to be expected that you will be able to complete every section of this chart at this stage. You may wish to revisit this as you proceed through the book and gather further evidence to support you in moving forward.

Section 1: Professional values and practice

STANDARD	WHAT DO I DO THAT MEETS THIS STANDARD? (LIST THE EVIDENCE THAT DEMONSTRATES THIS.)	WHAT ELSE DO I NEED TO DO TO MEET THIS STANDARD FULLY?
1.1 They have high expectations of all pupils; respect their social, cultural, linguistic, religious and ethnic backgrounds; and are committed to raising their educational achievement.		
1.2 They build and maintain successful relationships with pupils, treat them consistently, with respect and consideration, and are concerned for their development as learners.		
1.3 They demonstrate and promote the positive values, attitudes and behaviour they expect from the pupils with whom they work.		
1.4 They work collaboratively with colleagues, and carry out their roles effectively, knowing when to seek help and advice.		
1.5 They are able to liaise sensitively and effectively with parents and carers, recognising their roles in pupils' learning.		
1.6 They are able to improve their own practice, including through observation, evaluation and discussion with colleagues.		

STANDARD	WHAT DO I DO THAT MEETS THIS STANDARD?	WHAT ELSE DO I NEED TO DO TO MEET THIS STANDARD FULLY?
2.1 They have sufficient understanding of their specialist area to support pupils' learning, and are able to acquire further knowledge to contribute effectively and with confidence to the classes in which they are involved.		
2.2 They are familiar with the school curriculum, the age-related expectations of pupils, the main teaching methods and the testing/examination frameworks in the subjects and age ranges in which they are involved.		
2.3 They understand the aims, content, teaching strategies and intended outcomes for the lessons in which they are involved, and understand the place of these in the related teaching programme.		
2.4 They know how to use ICT to advance pupils' learning, and can use common ICT tools for their own and pupils' benefit.		
2.5 They know the key factors that can affect the way pupils learn.		
2.6 (a) They have achieved a qualification in English/ literacy equivalent to at least Level 2 of the National Qualifications Framework.		

Section 2 continued

2.6 (b) They have achieved a qualification in mathematics/numeracy equivalent to at least Level 2 of the National Qualifications Framework.		
2.7 They are aware of the statutory frameworks relevant to their role.		
2.8 They know the legal definition of Special Education Needs (SEN), and are familiar with the guidance about meeting SEN given in the SEN Code of Practice.		
2.9 They know a range of strategies to establish a purposeful learning environment and to promote good behaviour.		

Section 3: Teaching and learning activities
        a) Planning and expectations

STANDARD	WHAT DO I DO THAT MEETS THIS STANDARD?	WHAT ELSE DO I NEED TO DO TO MEET THIS STANDARD FULLY?
3.1.1 They contribute effectively to teachers' planning and preparation of lessons.		
3.1.2 Working within a framework set by the teacher, they plan their role in lessons, including how they will provide feedback to pupils and colleagues on pupils' learning and behaviour.		

Section 3 continued

3.1.3 They contribute effectively to the selection and preparation of teaching resources that meet the diversity of pupils' needs and interests.		
3.1.4 They are able to contribute to the planning of opportunities for pupils to learn in out-of-school contexts, in accordance with school policies and procedures.		

Section 3: Teaching and learning activities
b) Monitoring and assessment

STANDARD	WHAT DO I DO THAT MEETS THIS STANDARD?	WHAT ELSE DO I NEED TO DO TO MEET THIS STANDARD FULLY?
3.2.1 They are able to support teachers in evaluating pupils' progress through a range of assessment activities.		
3.2.2 They monitor pupils' responses to learning tasks and modify their approach accordingly.		
3.2.3 They monitor pupils' participation and progress, providing feedback to teachers, and giving constructive support to pupils as they learn.		
3.2.4 They contribute to maintaining and analysing records of pupils' progress.		

Section 3: Teaching and learning activities
  c) Teaching and learning activities

STANDARD	WHAT DO I DO THAT MEETS THIS STANDARD?	WHAT ELSE DO I NEED TO DO TO MEET THIS STANDARD FULLY?
3.3.1 Using clearly structured teaching and learning activities; they interest and motivate pupils, and advance their learning.		
3.3.2 They communicate effectively and sensitively with pupils to support their learning.		
3.3.3 They promote and support the inclusion of all pupils in the learning activities in which they are involved.		
3.3.4 They use behaviour management strategies, in line with the school's policy and procedures, which contribute to a purposeful learning environment.		
3.3.5 (a) They advance pupils' learning in a range of classroom settings, including working with individual pupils.		
3.3.5 (b) They advance pupils' learning in a range of classroom settings, including working with small groups of pupils.		
3.3.5 (c) They advance pupils' learning in a range of classroom settings, including working with whole classes where the assigned teacher is not present.		

3.3.6 They are able, where relevant, to guide the work of other adults supporting teaching and learning in the classroom.		
3.3.7 They recognise and respond effectively to equal opportunities issues as they arise, including by challenging stereotyped views, and by challenging bullying or harassment, following relevant policies and procedures.		
3.3.8 They organise and manage safely the learning activities, the physical teaching space and resources for which they are given responsibility.		

Having completed this task you may choose to approach the other chapters in this book either by selecting those which deal with topics where you feel you need most help, or by working gradually through the whole book and returning from time to time to these charts to assess your own progress. Whichever approach you adopt, I wish you well as you proceed towards your assessment.

At the end of this book, in Appendix 1, you will find a series of exemplars related to the response forms for the tasks which you will be required to undertake for assessment for the HLTA. Having completed your self-review against the standards this will help you to provide the examples for each of the four tasks. These tasks are:

● Task 1: working with an individual pupil;
● Task 2: working with a small group;
● Task 3: working with a whole class;
● Task 4: analysis of five situations or events.

For each of Tasks 1–3 above you will need to demonstrate:

- how you worked with the teacher to plan your contributions;
- your own planning for the work;
- how you carried out the work;
- how you evaluated your personal learning.

Once you have identified an appropriate example you need to keep a copy of all relevant documents and complete a response sheet for the task and then complete the assessment grid. Examples demonstrating this process are to be seen in Appendix 1.

Most candidates use Task 4 to cover those standards that are not clearly demonstrated in the other tasks. The response sheet for this task is different from that for the previous three and has the following sections:

- a brief description of the situation or event;
- a discussion of what occurred and why;
- a section in which you identify your learning points.

Summary

- There are two main routes into HLTA and you need to consider carefully which is most appropriate for you.
- The support of your school and colleagues is essential in enabling you to progress smoothly through this process.
- To be awarded HLTA status you will need to complete a series of assessments which indicate that you have achieved the standards.

References

Department for Education and Skills (2001) *Special educational needs code of practice*. London: DfES.

Teacher Training Agency (2004) *Professional standards for higher level teaching assistants*. London: TTA.

Teacher Training Agency (2005) *Meeting the professional standards for the award of the higher level teaching assistant status: guidance to the standards*. London: TTA.

2. Working with professional colleagues and others in the classroom

Introduction

While in the past many teachers have found themselves working alone in classrooms and, in some instances, viewed the classroom as their own domain, it is now much more usual to find that classrooms are managed by teams of people, who must all share the common purpose of meeting the needs of all pupils within a class. While teachers maintain overall responsibility for classroom management, it is now recognised that effective teaching is often dependent upon a number of individual professionals performing discrete but complementary roles. Research has indicated that many teachers now regard the role of the teaching assistant as a critical one in enabling them to address the needs of a diverse classroom population (Balshaw 1999, Rose 2001). The professionalism with which this role is carried out is therefore a critical factor in determining effective teaching. This demands that teaching assistants develop a level of skill and understanding which will enable them to carry out their duties in way which is fully supportive of the teaching and learning process. An important part of this role is the development of an appreciation of how working as part of a team may have an impact upon the quality of education provided to children in a class. The effective teaching assistant will understand the ways in which they may best provide support to both teachers and pupils in a range of situations.

There may, of course, be many other professional colleagues who work alongside teachers and teaching assistants in classrooms. These may include therapists who attend infrequently to address the needs of specific pupils with special educational needs, or specialist teachers, for example those working with pupils for whom English is an additional language. The professional teaching assistant can play a crucial role in enabling these colleagues to perform their duties efficiently and to have maximum effect upon those pupils who need this form of support. Working with such colleagues needs some understanding of their roles and responsibilities and also demands the acquisition of skills and understanding about how working as part of a classroom team may have benefits for all learners.

In addition to professional colleagues, it is likely that most classrooms will from time to time receive some support from volunteers and parents who come into school with a desire to offer help to the teacher. These individuals can play an important part in enabling the class teacher to manage the classroom. The role of the professional teaching assistant may be essential in ensuring that such help is carefully managed and has a positive impact upon the classroom environment and the learning of pupils.

In this chapter we will consider how the teaching assistant can develop the necessary skills and understanding to work alongside professional colleagues and others in the classroom. An opportunity will be provided to consider the roles of different individuals who may be encountered in the classroom and to examine those conditions which encourage effective teamwork for the support of all pupils. In particular, this chapter will focus upon the standards highlighted in the box below.

HLTA STANDARDS

1.4 They work collaboratively with colleagues, and carry out their roles effectively, knowing when to seek help and advice.

3.1.2 Working within a framework set by the teacher, they plan their role in lessons, including how they will provide feedback to pupils and colleagues on pupils' learning and behaviour.

3.3.6 They are able, where relevant, to guide the work of other adults supporting teaching and learning in the classroom.

CHAPTER OBJECTIVES

By the end of this chapter you should:

● appreciate the various roles played by adults in the classroom and the impact these have upon teaching and learning;

● have identified how your own role can be developed to ensure that you provide the most effective support for the class teacher, and how this role complements that of other professionals;

● have considered your role in managing volunteers, parents and other adults who are in class in a supportive role.

Understanding the teacher's role

Those professional colleagues with whom the teaching assistant is likely to spend most time will inevitably be teachers. The role of the teacher is both complex and multi-faceted and has, in recent years, become increasingly demanding as expectations of pupil performance and assessment against national standards has become paramount. Dean (1992) identified 12 tasks which she saw as critical components of the teacher's role, these being:

● the observation of children;
● organisation of the learning programme;
● the selection of learning material;
● the presentation of learning material;
● matching work to children;

- the structuring of children's learning;
- training learning behaviour;
- providing inspiration and encouragement;
- organising a learning environment;
- ensuring that children develop a common understanding with the teacher;
- assessing and recording children's progress and development;
- assessing teaching performance and approaches.

(Dean 1992, pp52–8)

Each of these 12 tasks makes considerable professional demands upon the teacher and can provide an indication of where carefully directed attention from a teaching assistant may be vital. The teacher has overall responsibility for the management of the class and the teaching assistant must work under their direction. However, as teachers have come to gain greater confidence in the skills of teaching assistants, so have they become more inclined to share their planning and delivery. Research conducted by Moyles (1997) indicated that traditionally the class teacher played a role which demanded that they rove around the classroom monitoring and orchestrating the work of all pupils, while the teaching assistant was more likely to play a static role working with small groups or individuals. More recently this perception has changed, with teachers and teaching assistants being encouraged to engage together in planning which enables the teaching assistant to assume greater responsibility for the delivery and assessment of parts of lessons to a wider variety of groups. Kerry (2000) emphasises that a teaching assistant in the classroom does not simply provide an extra pair of hands. They should also provide the opportunity for teachers to make use of their experience, expertise and ideas at all stages of the teaching process. Inevitably teachers and teaching assistants will see situations from differing perspectives. So long as a confident and positive relationship exists between these two roles, these differing views can be used to support the development of teaching and learning in a positive manner.

Attempting to understand the classroom situation from the teacher's perspective is an important process. It is one through which the teaching assistant may develop their own skill in understanding the important relationship between what the teacher does and the intended learning outcomes. Just as effective teachers are always questioning their own approaches and making adjustments in order to become more effective (Day 1999), so must the professional teaching assistant learn to reflect upon their own performance. Teachers learn to adapt to a wide range of teaching situations and environments. Not all situations demand the same approaches or response and the most effective teachers learn to adjust their behaviour as different circumstances demand. This flexibility comes, to some extent, with experience but also requires that teachers reflect upon their own performance and are willing to try new ideas and change established practices. It is equally important that teaching assistants adopt this flexible approach.

Effective communication between the teacher and the teaching assistant is paramount in ensuring that effective teamwork is achieved. Teachers will gain confidence in the teaching assistants with whom they work when they recognise that they have the professional skills needed to work effectively in their classroom. Each teacher is an individual and will have their own preferred ways of working. Therefore it is important that the teaching assistant gains as clear a view as possible of the teacher's expectations and the ways in which they wish to work. Demonstrating flexibility as well as professional competence may well be an essential factor in gaining teacher confidence. The easiest way to gain a full appreciation of the expectation of a teacher with whom you will work is clearly to have a discussion centred upon the management of the classroom. However, this will be most productive if you provide a structure that enables you to engage in a conversation which addresses the most important aspects of the teacher's work. Dean's list of 12 teacher tasks presented earlier in this chapter can provide a useful framework for gaining an understanding of how teachers perceive their role and how you may best support them in achieving the results which they seek. The following practical activity which has condensed the issues raised by Dean, is designed to assist you in gaining an understanding of teacher expectations and also to enable you to demonstrate your own professional skills and understanding to the teacher.

PRACTICAL TASK

In order to complete this task effectively you will need to negotiate two blocks of time to spend in discussion with the teacher. Once this has been agreed this task is best undertaken in a relaxed and comfortable environment, possibly over a cup of tea or coffee.

Be clear with the teacher that the purpose of this task is to gain a clearer understanding of how the teacher perceives their role and how you can be most effective in supporting them in the classroom. *Before* the meeting, give the teacher the list of questions to be asked in order that they are clear about the focus of the discussion.

Engage the teacher in a discussion based upon the following questions. If the teacher is willing, make a tape-recording of the discussion. If the teacher is not willing to be recorded, then make notes related to each of the questions.

- What are the most important preparations you have to make before a lesson?

- How do you decide what work each pupil or group of pupils will undertake?

- How do you decide the ways in which you will group pupils?

- What do you do to ensure that all pupils are learning?

- How do you decide what to assess and how to do it?

If you require clarification of any points from the teacher's answers, be confident in asking for this as you go along through the discussion. After each of these questions, ask the teacher 'In what ways can my role as teaching assistant make this task more effective?'

When the discussion has finished, go through the recording (or your notes) carefully. Make a series of bullet points highlighting the issues raised in the response to each question. List your own ideas for how you see your role in supporting the teacher and take these back to the teacher for further discussion. Ask the teacher if your perception of their role and the ways in which you feel you can be most effective in providing support agrees with their own ideas. Where there is agreement, talk about how you might put actions into place in the classroom. If there are disagreements discuss where and why these exist.

In an ideal world the teacher and teaching assistant would always agree about how their roles may complement each other. However, as we do not work in such ideal circumstances it is inevitable that from time to time we will need to compromise in order to maintain an effective working partnership. By going through this task with the teacher, the teaching assistant is demonstrating a preparedness to understand the complex role of the teacher and is offering personal insights into this role and the ways in which it may be supported. This is an important process in beginning to share in the development of professional respect and confidence.

In the classroom situation teachers are responsible overall for the management of teaching and learning and all that this entails. While teachers are responsible for the direction of others in the classroom, it is, as we have already seen, only one part of their job. At times the teaching assistant may feel that they are not given sufficient guidance by the teacher or that they need more specific advice with regards to managing an individual or group of pupils. Most teachers will be only too pleased to provide this support but can only do so when they are aware of the situation. Sometimes this support is not provided because the teacher has assumed that all is well and they have every confidence in what you are doing. When seeking advice it is important to be clear about both situations and problems. If you are having difficulties or do not understand what is expected of you, be prepared to:

- describe which parts of a task or situation are of concern to you;
- say why these are of concern;
- ask advice on how to proceed;
- check that the actions which you are going to take are appropriate and meet the teacher's expectations.

Quite often this kind of clarification will only be possible at the end of a lesson or at the end of the day. However, it is essential that such a discussion does take place in order that actions may be changed before a similar situation arises in the future. Professional teamwork is built upon mutual respect and understanding.

This will only be achieved upon the basis of professional discussions of this nature. Each participant in a partnership must demonstrate professional respect for the others (Mills and Mills 1995, Lacey 2001) and this will only be achieved when each partner attempts to see a situation from the point of view of the other. The professional classroom assistant will learn to ask for clarification, and also seek reasoning behind the advice given. Effective teachers will want to provide the most supportive learning environment possible and will welcome an opportunity to ensure that their expectations are clear.

The teaching assistant will gain increased confidence from the teacher as they demonstrate their understanding of the needs of pupils and offer their own opinions of how to address these.

Case study

Michael is a teaching assistant working in a junior school. Every Tuesday afternoon he supports a teacher in a PE lesson with a mixed years 5 and 6 class. During today's lesson Michael was asked to supervise a group of eight pupils in developing a floor exercise sequence. While most of the pupils in the group appeared enthusiastic and confident in this activity, one girl, Melanie, was particularly difficult and did not want to join in. As the class teacher was busy supervising an activity with the rest of the group, Michael did not feel that he could ask for immediate advice. In order to ensure that the session ran smoothly, Michael asked Melanie to assist him in assessing how well the others were performing their floor exercises. This she was happy to do, offering comments on how the other pupils could improve upon their individual performances.

Michael felt that while his strategy had succeeded in enabling the lesson to continue effectively, Melanie had not participated as the class teacher would have wanted. At the end of the lesson he discussed the situation with the teacher, explaining the situation and the actions that he had taken.

The class teacher listened to Michael and considered that the actions which he had taken were wholly appropriate to the situation. In order to move the situation forward he suggested that next week Michael might begin by giving the same role to Melanie but, after a while, ask her to demonstrate to one of the pupils how they might improve upon their performance.

In the case study above we see an example of a teaching assistant using his own initiative to address an immediate problem when the teacher could not be consulted. By explaining clearly to the teacher both the situation and the way in which he dealt with this, Michael has gained the teacher's confidence and has demonstrated his professional approach. He has also provided the teacher with an opportunity to build upon his actions and to have the confidence that Michael will be able to manage the situation effectively in the next PE lesson.

Working with other professional colleagues

Schools often work as part of a multi-disciplinary service in an attempt to adopt holistic approaches to the management of pupils. In your work as a teaching assistant you are likely to come into contact with a wide range of professional colleagues. These may include social workers, therapists – such as speech and language therapists – psychologists or teachers from a special educational needs support service. Each one of these professionals has a distinct and important role to play in enabling pupils to work effectively in school and, where necessary, to overcome obstacles to learning. Teaching assistants can play a vital part in ensuring that the work of these professional colleagues has a positive impact on pupils. Lacey (2001) has demonstrated that one of the most important features of effective teamwork is the establishment of trust. It is critical that members working within a collaborative teaching situation have confidence in all team members. Demonstrating your professionalism is important in gaining trust and contributing positively to a team effort.

All professional colleagues must work within a strict code of ethics which is designed to protect pupils, professional colleagues and parents. You will have access to information about children and families which may be sensitive and which you must keep confidential at all times. Casual conversations both inside and outside of school can, in an unguarded moment, lead to disclosures about children or families which could have a detrimental effect upon them. You must ensure that you are constantly vigilant to protect the rights of all members of the school community.

There are important principles to which all effective team members must adhere, these include:

- **Respecting confidentiality**: often you will be privy to information about pupils, which must remain confidential. For example, as part of a professional team you may have access to written or oral information about a pupil's home situation. This information may be essential to the way in which this pupil is managed, but should not be shared with anyone outside of the classroom team.
- **Respecting professional expertise**: each member of a professional team has a specialist and unique contribution to make. For example, the speech and language therapist will have skills and knowledge that are associated with their profession. This must be respected and advice given with regard to the speech and language needs of pupils should be listened to and acted upon.
- **Ensuring understanding**: it is sometimes easy for professionals to be so focused upon their area of expertise that they forget that others may not understand their ways of thinking. Good teams in classrooms avoid using excessive jargon and accept the need for explanation when questioned about terminology or approaches. Never be afraid to ask for clarification; it does not show your ignorance but rather demonstrates your professionalism.

As a professional teaching assistant you may often be asked to carry out work set or organised by a professional colleague who makes only occasional visits to school. For example, a member of the special educational needs support service might provide a programme for a pupil to help them achieve a target related to their Individual Education Plan (IEP). A class teacher may direct you to carry out the programme with the pupil, either in an individual teaching session or during group activity. It is important that you follow the instructions provided in a way that has maximum benefits for the pupil. The following checklist might assist you in this situation.

- Check that you understand what is expected of you in delivering the programme.
- Familiarise yourself before the session with any materials or equipment which you might have to use.
- Clarify with the teacher or the professional colleague who supplied the programme what the expected outcomes of your work with the pupil should be.
- Check what you are supposed to record from the session and how this should be fed back to the teacher or other professional colleagues.

In many classes you may find that it is unusual to work with professional colleagues other than the class teacher. However, it is important that you are prepared for this situation to arise and familiarise yourself with the roles of specific professionals.

It is unlikely in most schools that you will find yourself working with all of these professional colleagues, but the more knowledgeable you are about their roles and their expectations of you, the easier it will be for you to contribute to their work for the benefit of individuals or groups of pupils.

Case study

Oskar is a pupil who joined St Patrick's Junior School at the start of this term, having arrived recently in England from Romania. When he first arrived in school he had only a few words of English and was very shy and apprehensive in school. After he had been in school for two weeks Oskar was visited by a teacher from the county multi-cultural education service who brought with her a lady who speaks Romanian. They conducted a series of tests which indicated that Oskar is a very bright boy who is eager to learn. They suggested that to help Oskar to learn he might enjoy playing a board game with some of the other pupils in the class. This game involves matching words to a series of pictures of objects that he will find around the classroom. The words are provided in both English and Romanian. Marianne, who is the teaching assistant in Oskar's class plays this game with him and a group of three or four other pupils each morning when he arrives in class. The English pupils enjoy the game because they are learning some Romanian words and Oskar is encouraged by them to improve his English.

Marianne has specific instructions from the multi-cultural service teacher, these are:

- *make the game fun;*
- *help Oskar by getting the other pupils to model their English when teaching him new words;*
- *correct his pronunciation – but make it fun;*
- *record the words which he is using consistently and those which he finds difficult;*
- *identify opportunities for Oskar to use the words at other times during the day.*

Marianne has agreed to give feedback to both the multi-cultural service teacher and his class teacher on Oskar's response to the game after a fortnight.

PRACTICAL TASK

Complete the following checklist in relation to the school in which you work. Where you cannot fill in the boxes, ask a teacher from the school for the information. Try to meet as many of the professionals who work in school as possible and find out from them what they see their role as being. It is possible that some of these professional colleagues may never visit your school.

PROFESSIONAL ROLE	DO I KNOW THEIR NAME?	DO I KNOW WHAT THEY DO?	DO I KNOW WHICH PUPILS THEY WORK WITH?
Special educational needs support teachers			
Speech and language therapist			
Physiotherapist			
Occupational therapist			
Education welfare officer			
Teacher from the multi-cultural service			
Social worker			
Educational psychologist			

Parents and volunteers in the classroom

Parents who visit classrooms to work with pupils must always be made welcome and feel comfortable in class. Most schools have clear policies about parent helpers and it is important that as a professional teaching assistant you are familiar with this policy. Some schools encourage parents to work in class alongside their own son or daughter, while others prefer them to work in a different class.

You should expect that parents are likely to see the role of the teacher and the teaching assistant as being distinctly different. It is probable that they will expect the teacher to have skills and competencies which you may not possess. This should not bother you – it is likely that many parents will not be sure about your role and may never have encountered a teaching assistant when they attended school! Teachers should always clarify your role to parents and introduce you as a professional colleague.

Parents entering a classroom may be apprehensive and unsure of what is expected. It is possible that you will be expected to take a role in managing their work and encouraging them to fit into class routines. For some parents you may be seen as less formidable than the teacher who they regard as the person in authority in the class. It is essential that you demonstrate your professionalism by clarifying to parents the ways in which you support the teacher and the responsibilities which you hold in the class. A particularly important part of your task with parents is to act as a role model in supporting pupils and demonstrating what is expected and how things are done.

There are important principles which you should follow when working with parents in school.

- Make them feel at ease, show them that you value their insights and ideas.
- Listen to what they have to say about pupils with whom they have worked in the class.
- When directing parents give clear instructions and check their understanding. If necessary demonstrate how to do things, including the use of equipment.
- Be aware of confidential information and cautious not to disclose information about pupils that their own parents may not wish to be known.
- Check what parent helpers have done and give feedback on this to them and the teacher.

Some parents may bring specific skills and expertise into the classroom, for example they may have artistic or musical talents or be proficient in using computers. The same may be true of volunteers. If they come to school to undertake specific tasks with pupils related to a particular talent or skill, the work which they undertake must be clarified with and directed by the teacher. Volunteers often need clear direction and here the teaching assistant may play a vital role. You will know the individual pupils better than the volunteer and should be in a position to advise them regarding how pupils may respond and any particular difficulties which they may encounter. As with directing parents, you need to give clear instructions and to monitor and evaluate their work and inform the teacher of any concerns which you might have.

Working with others in the classroom is not always easy. All teams face the challenge of getting along together and working towards common goals, often through stressful situations. One ineffective team member can change the whole way in which the team functions. It is important that you spend time considering what impact your actions have upon the efficiency of the class teams with which you operate.

Summary

Collaborative work is dependent upon:

- effective communication between team members;
- a clear understanding of and respect for the role of other colleagues;
- carefully articulated information to appropriate team members and particularly the class teacher about the performance of pupils or the effectiveness of strategies used to support pupils;
- maintenance of good records;
- the provision of clear directions to other adults when necessary.

References

Balshaw, M (1999) *Help in the classroom* (2nd edn) London: David Fulton.

Day, C (1999) Researching teaching through reflective practice, in Loughran, J (ed) *Researching teaching*. London: Falmer.

Dean, J (1992) *Organising learning in the primary classroom*. London: Routledge.

Kerry, T (2000) *Working with support staff*. (2nd edn) London: Pearson Education.

Lacey, P (2001) *Support partnerships: collaboration in action*. London: David Fulton.

Mills, J and Mills, RW (1995) *Primary school people: getting to know your colleagues*. London: Routledge.

Moyles, J (1997) *Jills of all trades*. London: ATL.

Rose, R (2001) Primary school teacher perceptions of the conditions required to include pupils with special educational needs. *Educational Review*, 53 (2): 147–56.

Introduction

The relationship between teaching and learning is at the heart of the education process. Each teacher and pupil is an individual and as such will have their own ideas and preferences with regards to teaching approaches and how they like to learn. It should never be assumed that because you have clear intended outcomes for a session that you teach this will necessarily be what pupils will learn. Each of us responds differently to learning situations. Some, for example, will enjoy learning in mathematics lessons and will respond to mathematical ideas with ease, while finding reading difficult; others will respond well in practical learning situations, while finding the accumulation of information from graphical representation difficult. Good teachers have recognised the challenges presented by these factors for a long time and have learned to plan their lessons in ways which address a range of preferred learning styles and which present opportunities for pupils to tackle learning in a variety of ways. Dean (1994) suggests that it is not always easy to define good teaching practice. Teachers may appear to be well organised and efficient but this in itself will not guarantee that pupils learn. Teaching and learning are complex processes that are subject to many social, cultural and economic influences. In order to succeed, effective teachers need to vary their teaching approaches, to be adaptable and to be vigilant in gauging how pupils respond to their teaching style, the resources they use and the environment in which they are working. As a professional teaching assistant you can play an important role in assisting the teachers with whom you work to manage the learning situation for the benefit of all pupils.

In this chapter we will consider the ways in which you, as a professional teaching assistant, can assist pupils in their learning through careful planning and preparation to meet a range of needs, aptitudes and abilities. Your attitudes and expectations can have a critical impact upon whether pupils feel comfortable with learning and can make a considerable difference to the progress which they make. Similarly, your expertise and professional approach should be an important ingredient in the teachers' ability to manage whole class and group teaching situations effectively. Through your observation of pupils, your analysis of how they are performing, and your discussions with teachers, you can make a crucial contribution to the effectiveness of learning in the classroom. This chapter will examine how you can ensure that your role makes a major contribution to the progress of every pupil in the classes in which you work. In particular this chapter will focus upon the standards highlighted in the box below:

HLTA STANDARDS

1.1 They have high expectations of all pupils; respect their social, cultural, linguistic, religious and ethnic backgrounds; and are committed to raising their educational achievement.

1.6 They are able to improve their own practice, including through observation, evaluation and discussion with colleagues.

2.2 They are familiar with the school curriculum, the age-related expectations of pupils, the main teaching methods and the testing/examination frameworks in the subjects and age ranges inwhich they are involved.

2.3 They understand the aims, content, teaching strategies and intended outcomes for the lessons in which they are involved, and understand the place of these in the related teaching programme.

2.5 They know the key factors that can affect the way pupils learn.

3.1.1 They contribute effectively to teachers' planning and preparation of lessons.

3.1.3 They contribute to the selection and preparation of teaching resources that meet the diversity of pupils' needs and interests.

3.2.2 They monitor pupils' responses to learning tasks and modify their approach accordingly.

3.2.3 They monitor pupils' participation and progress, providing feedback to teachers, and giving constructive support to pupils as they learn.

3.2.4 They contribute to maintaining and analysing records of pupils' progress.

3.3.1 Using clearly structured teaching and learning activities, they interest and motivate pupils, and advance their learning.

3.3.2 They communicate effectively and sensitively with pupils to support their learning.

3.3.6 They are able, where relevant, to guide the work of other adults supporting teaching and learning in the classroom.

3.3.8 They organise and manage safely the learning activities, the physical teaching space and resources for which they are given responsibility.

CHAPTER OBJECTIVES

By the end of this chapter you should:

● be aware of your school's strategies for the promotion of effective teaching and learning;

● have considered approaches to effective planning of the teaching sessions which you manage;

● be aware of factors which influence the success and failure of pupils' learning;

● have an understanding of strategies which you may use to promote effective learning for a diverse range of pupils.

What do we mean by learning?

Learning takes place when children can do, understand or know something which previously they could not achieve or did not know. While much of what is learned in schools comes from the formal process of teaching, there is much which pupils learn that can be described as incidental or for which no direct planning takes place. In addition to learning about subjects or developing specific skills in school, pupils engage in learning as a social process through which they engage with others, learning how to play a role as a member of a team and collaborating in solving problems. This is an important part of learning and provides a foundation for pupils to become effective learners. Learning the skills of participation, co-operation and teamwork are critical elements in the classroom. Pupils who can work in social situations usually prosper in school more than those who find it difficult to form relationships and collaborate with others. This is not to say that working independently is not important. Effective learners can adjust to a variety of teaching approaches and learning situations. In most classrooms pupils will encounter a wide variety of such situations and opportunities. These will typically include whole class teaching, small group work, paired work and even individual sessions working with an adult. Not all pupils will respond equally well to each of these situations and it is important that teachers are aware of how pupils respond in different circumstances. As a professional teaching assistant you can play an important role in observing pupil reactions and noting how they respond in a range of situations. Pollard and Tann (1991) have emphasised the importance of talking to pupils about how they prefer to learn and about their understanding of teacher expectations. Teaching assistants are often in a position to engage pupils in such conversations and may well gain insights into pupils' preferred learning styles which will support teachers in planning for future lessons.

Good teachers are able to identify those critical components of what is being taught which pupils must master in order to make progress. They are aware that pupils need to develop skills at one point in their learning which will ensure that they can make progress later on. Some pupils who have difficulties with learning will need longer than others to acquire these core skills and are likely to need additional support. Teaching assistants often find themselves working with pupils who are having difficulties learning what others in the class may be achieving with fewer problems. In such situations pupils can easily become demotivated or anxious that they are falling behind their peers. You may be able to play an important role in giving additional attention and support to pupils in this situation. However, it is important to do so in a manner which does not add to the pupil's anxieties. You must draw upon the pupil's learning strengths, ensuring that you emphasise what the pupil can do rather than pointing out their difficulties. You may also need to try several ways of teaching the pupil rather than continually using one method which the pupil finds difficult. Part of this process is about knowing the pupils with whom you work and recognising how they respond to a range of teaching situations.

PRACTICAL TASK

Select four pupils of differing abilities in a class with which you have regular contact. In the boxes provided make a few notes about how you think they respond to the different teaching situations listed.

- Which approach do you think they prefer?
- In which situations do they work well?
- Why do you think they work well, or not so well, in these situations?

After you have completed this chart, talk to each of the pupils and ask them about their preferred approaches.

- Does the preferred approach depend upon the subject, the teacher, the other pupils in a group, or other factors?
- How did your perceptions match those of the pupils?
- How might you use this information when planning activities with these pupils?

PUPIL	WHOLE CLASS TEACHING	GROUP WORK	PAIRED WORK	INDIVIDUAL TAUGHT SESSIONS	WORKING ALONE

What are the factors that influence learning?

Pupils learn effectively when they feel confident, assured about the materials they are using and comfortable with the people they are learning with and by whom they are being taught. Pupils have very clear views about what can help them to learn. Burke and Grosvenor (2003) sought the opinions of pupils about the kind of school which they would like. In the section of their book which deals with learning, pupils articulate their understanding of the constraints under which teachers often have to work and express their views about what encourages them to work well. They are clearly concerned that they should be challenged and respected as learners, that they respond to teachers and other adults who are interested in them and engage them in a positive manner. All learners need to be motivated and this begins with establishing a relationship between teacher and learner which is based upon mutual trust, interest and respect. Pupils do not come to lessons as empty vessels to be filled with knowledge; they bring with them their own interests and experiences which make effective starting points for learning. A pupil who is having difficulties with the contents of a lesson is likely to 'switch off' unless they can see that it has direct relevance to them. Teaching assistants can often play an important role in providing a personal focus for pupils in lessons. This may involve encouraging them by reminding them of previous successes in lessons, or taking the lesson materials and relating these to the pupil's own experiences or interests.

Case study

Wayne is a year 4 pupil who finds learning in mathematics lessons particularly difficult. At times in these lessons, when he is struggling to complete work, he can become disruptive and this results in his being told off by the teacher. In today's lesson Wayne's class are working on probability. They have played games with dice and with cards and now they are being asked to solve a number of problems using their understanding of probability. While the other pupils on Wayne's table are getting on well with the tasks set, he is having difficulties with the work and has given up trying. Alison, the TA in the class, has noticed this and tries to help him with his work. Wayne is reluctant to co-operate until Alison changes the nature of the task. She knows that Wayne is a fan of the local football team. With the agreement of the teacher she asks Wayne to list the names of all the players in his favourite team. She then does an exercise with him looking at how he can make decisions about the probability of each player scoring a goal during the next three matches. Wayne is far more interested in this activity than the one set and can now see the relevance of what he is doing. After working on this for a while, Alison redirects Wayne to the original task and helps him to see how he can transfer what he has been doing with his football team back to the task set by the teacher.

The case study presented above only works if a number of conditions are in place. First, Alison has a good relationship with Wayne. He trusts her and is prepared to listen to what she says. Furthermore, Alison knows about Wayne's interests and has sufficient subject understanding to be able to adjust his work in order to deal with the required mathematical learning in a way which interests Wayne. It is important that such approaches are undertaken with the consent of the teacher. It is equally important that after the initial engagement with Wayne, Alison redirects him to the required task. Here we can see Alison playing a vital role in preventing disruptive behaviour, raising the self-esteem of the learner and supporting the teacher by maintaining a focus upon the core learning of the lesson.

All pupils require feedback on how they are doing. Barnes (1999) has coined the phrase *descriptive praise* to describe the ways in which teachers and others can offer encouragement to pupils. All pupils like to be praised, but Barnes suggests that simply saying 'Well done' or 'That's brilliant' is insufficiently focused to help the pupil advance in their learning. Pupils are more motivated if you describe why you are offering praise. For example, 'That really is an excellent piece of writing, well done. I like it because you have created the atmosphere of a dark house on a windy night and I can really imagine what it is like to be there. That's really good work'. Here the pupil is left in no doubt about what is being praised and why. This is much more likely to encourage the pupil to maintain the level of work and also helps them to focus upon those characteristics of their writing which you perceive as positive.

There are, of course, other factors which influence learning and sometimes these may be beyond your control. The materials and resources provided for pupils are important. Learners like to work with interesting and accessible materials. The availability of these may determine the ways in which you group pupils (*see* Chapter 4) or the type of teaching approach which you adopt. Pupils need to learn to share equipment but if you are managing a group of pupils all of whom need to use a piece of apparatus to complete a task and you have only one of these to share between six pupils, if they all require the equipment at the same time, you may have difficulties managing the group. Before any activity think about the materials and resources you will use and how you will organise the activity to minimise disruption. Try to prevent pupils having to do nothing while they wait for the equipment. Plan a series of tasks within the main activity, which means that they always have something to do.

Of equal importance is the learning environment in which pupils have to work. Not all classrooms are well designed, though much can be done to create a positive learning environment. When managing groups of pupils think about where they are to be located. What are the distractions in this area and can any of them be minimised? For example, if you are working by a window and there is a football match taking place outside, can you seat the pupils in such a position that they are not distracted by events on the field? Is there enough space for pupils to complete the task which they have been given?

Some practical lessons, such as art, may require considerable space in order for pupils to work efficiently. Think about the space needed for a lesson and how you will position pupils to help them work efficiently without getting in each other's way. Sometimes you can help by ensuring that pupils have only the materials required for a specific part of a task rather than having lots of superfluous materials which clutter a table or work area. All learners work more effectively when they are comfortable.

Many schools have recognised the importance of giving pupils a balance of activities. Some lessons in school of necessity demand that pupils are quite sedentary. They may be required to sit at tables for prolonged periods and to engage in activities which require them to work at a table. This is, of course, perfectly acceptable in relation to many of the lessons which teachers manage in today's classrooms. However, all pupils will benefit from changes of learning situation. Encouraging pupils to do some physical exercise between lessons or even during a lesson will prove beneficial for most learners. Think about your own working patterns. Most adults soon tire of working at one activity for extended periods. If you have been working at a computer for some time and grow tired of this you do not regain your enthusiasm simply by engaging in another computer activity. Pupils need this change of learning emphasis and will appreciate opportunities to move between activities which are relatively passive and those which demand that they move about much more.

Planning and preparation for effective teaching and learning

Managing the learning situation and environment

Good preparation is essential in enabling all classroom managers, including yourself as a teaching assistant, to ensure that learning can take place. When working with a group of pupils you will need to consider how you position pupils in a group, how you manage the distractions which may impede learning, the choice of teaching materials and the pace of the work which you undertake with pupils. Before you commence your session with a group of pupils you should ask a number of critical questions which may enable you to create a good learning environment. These will include:

- Do I have all of the resources and materials, which I need for this session?
- Are these materials and resources suitable for everyone in the group?
- Am I clear about the intended outcomes of the session?
- Where will I be working and do I need to arrange furniture or other parts of the learning environment?
- What will I do if the pupils finish this activity more quickly than I had expected?
- What am I expected to observe, assess and report to the teacher?

These questions should enable you to enter a teaching session with the confidence that you will succeed in supporting pupils effectively and be able to enjoy your teaching session.

The management of resources is an important factor in encouraging the lesson to run smoothly. If pupils constantly have to leave their work to fetch rulers or rubbers or collect other materials they become a distraction to others and a potential source of disruption. Pupils need to have easy access to those materials which you expect they will use. If pupils are being expected to share resources, such as reference books or a piece of science equipment, then provide them with rules and guidelines about how this will be managed. Try to break your session down into parts so that not all resources are required at the same time by all pupils.

Just as a lack of resources can cause difficulties with classroom management, so can too many become a distraction. Pupils will often find difficulties in resisting the temptation to play with interesting materials which are in front of them and become distracted from what you intend they should be doing. Make sure that you have all the resources to hand that you will need for a lesson, but that pupils are given these only when they are needed. In this way they will focus upon those resources which you want them to be using, and are less likely to wander off task.

Before you begin your session consider the needs and abilities of the pupils in your group. If you have pupils with special educational needs or others for whom English is an additional language, what are the challenges they will face in this particular session? Do you need to differentiate your approach to ensure that these pupils can participate fully? (*See* Chapter 8.) Attempting to make adjustments during the session will almost certainly add to your stresses and be less effective than being well organised beforehand.

Whenever you are teaching you should be clear in your mind about what outcomes are expected from the lesson. Once you have determined this you will find it easier to assess the progress which is being made and to understand how you may need to alter the pace of your lesson or modify your expectations of pupils. Good teachers will communicate their intentions to you, including ideas for how you may address the diverse needs of the pupils in your group. Not all pupils will be working at the same pace, neither is it likely that they will all require the same outcomes. Communicating your expectations to the pupils, in a way that enables them to monitor their own progress and understand the sequence of events in a lesson, is important. When pupils are clear about these matters, they are more likely to move smoothly towards a successful outcome. You can also prevent anxiety on the part of those learners who are not likely to achieve as much during the lesson as some of their more able peers by making them aware of your expectations which are specific to them.

In this chapter we have already considered the importance of eliminating distraction in the learning environment. Do not be afraid to ask pupils critical questions about how they best learn. Pupils can often identify those conditions which support their learning. By giving them an opportunity to discuss who they work best with, or how they want part of the classroom arranged for a lesson, you will discover more about those conditions which are conducive to effective learning. Clearly, if you know of pupils who do not get on well together, or others who are likely to distract their friends from working, this may influence the ways in which you arrange the learning environment. Once you have determined how you want to set up part of the room for an activity, try to do this before the teaching begins as this will be far less distracting and will not take away valuable time from learning.

At times, even the best-organised teachers find difficulties with timing an activity. Many factors can influence how long an activity or lesson takes. This may include the mood or energy levels of the pupils, the complexity of concepts being taught, the materials being used, or unexpected events and distractions which occur during a lesson. Teachers often report their frustration at not completing work set for a lesson. However, a greater concern often arises when pupils complete work more quickly than had been expected. As a professional teaching assistant you will often find yourself in a situation where a teacher has set the work and your role is to complete this with the pupils. When this work is completed more quickly than expected, you may find yourself with a period of time at the end of a lesson which you need to fill. If you have had an opportunity to consider the lesson well in advance, you may be able to design a short related activity which you could use to fill in time at the end of the lesson. However, in some circumstances you will have had insufficient time or notice of the activity to be this well prepared. Many experienced teachers find it helpful to have a range of pre-prepared activities in hand for just such an occasion. In some instances this may be something as simple as a story related to the topic of work, in others it could be a game or activity which reinforces learning from a lesson earlier in the week. It is worth considering the development of a bank of such activities which may enable you to avoid difficulties in such situations.

Observing what happens and sharing information

When working with a group of pupils you will need to be able to observe what happens during the session and to be able to feed information back to the teacher in a way which is helpful to them. Wragg (1999) has emphasised the many uses of classroom observation which may aid the teaching process. He is very aware of the challenges, which face all professionals in busy classrooms, and does not suggest that systematic observation is something which may easily be achieved. However, he does discuss the importance of observation as part of an evaluative process which informs teachers and others of what has happened and how they may have a more positive impact upon pupils' learning. Before a lesson begins, the teacher should have communicated their expectations with respect to learning outcomes and the needs of individual pupils. You should also have an opportunity to discuss with the teacher those important aspects of the lesson which the teacher requires you to observe and record. In some instances this may relate to the use of specific resources and how pupils interact with these, on other occasions you may focus upon the interactions of an individual pupil within a specific group. You will not, realistically, have a lot of time to conduct formal observations during your teaching session. However, some preparation beforehand may enable you to provide critical information for the teacher. A pro forma, such as the one provided here may assist you with this process.

Lesson:
Intended outcomes:
Pupil performance:
Other comments:

The following example is taken from an evaluation of a geography session conducted by a teaching assistant in a junior school. She had been asked specifically to comment on how the pupils worked together during this session.

Lesson: Identifying features from around the village on an ordnance survey map. Making a map of a fictitious village and locating symbols on the map. Explaining why these features are important in a village.
Intended outcomes: Pupils should be able to identify the map symbols from the key on the map. Pupils will justify why they locate features in a village and what advantages these bring to the villagers.
Pupil performance: Pupils enjoyed the activity. Most were able to name the symbols for church with a tower, telephone box, post office and picnic place from the village. There were insufficient maps for the whole group to share properly during the first part of the lesson. Some pupils did not share well but the pupils worked better in pairs designing their own village.
Other comments: More time was needed to complete the work on designing a village. We did not have enough time to discuss why they had put features in the village.

Here the teaching assistant has provided information which could help the teacher in planning to follow up on this lesson. She has also provided useful critical commentary on the need to resource the activity and about lesson timings. Not all lessons will be evaluated in this detail: often at the end of the lesson a teaching assistant will simply provide verbal feedback to the teacher. However, the advantage of a simple system such as that demonstrated above, is that it provides a record for the teacher and encourages the teaching assistant to give attention to a specific area of detail which may have a positive impact upon teaching and learning.

In addition to telling the teaching assistant and the teacher something about the performance of the pupils or the effectiveness of resources, such evaluative processes can also provide an opportunity for self-reflection on performance and may enable you to consider how you may change your own teaching approach or develop your classroom management skills.

Summary

Planning for teaching and learning is dependent upon:

- good communication between the teacher and teaching assistant;
- careful consideration and organisation of the classroom environment and learning resources;
- a good understanding of intended learning outcomes;
- effective use of resources;
- regular evaluation of how pupils are performing;
- a critical self-evaluation of performance.

References

Barnes, R (1999) *Positive teaching, positive learning*. London: Routledge.

Burke, C and Grosvenor, I (2003) *The school I'd like*. London: Routledge Falmer.

Dean, J (1994) *Organising learning in the primary classroom*. London: Routledge.

Pollard, A and Tann, S (1991) *Reflective teaching in the primary school*. London: Cassell.

Wragg, EC (1999) *An introduction to classroom observation*. (2nd edn) London: Routledge.

4. Managing groups of diverse need and ability

Introduction

Within any classroom you will encounter pupils who have a wide range of needs, motivation and ability. You will find some pupils who appear to find learning easy, while others seem to struggle to grasp even the most fundamental concepts. A major challenge for the teacher is to be able to address these diverse needs in every lesson. Teaching assistants often find themselves working with groups of pupils of mixed ability and therefore need to develop some of the teacher's skills in being able to meet a range of needs. This means having some understanding about how pupil needs are identified, how learning objectives are established and how careful planning can ensure that a range of needs and abilities are met within a single session.

In this chapter we will examine these issues and offer some practical advice on working in group situations. Particular consideration will be given to a range of approaches to differentiating learning in groups, and to enabling you to support the demands made upon teachers to ensure that all pupils are engaged with learning at an appropriate level. Clearly it is the teacher's responsibility to ensure that activities are planned effectively so as to meet the needs of all pupils in the class. Inevitably, from time to time, you will find yourself working with a group of pupils where one or more are either struggling with the task set, or find the work insufficiently challenging. This is not a criticism of the teacher who sets the work because meeting the needs of all pupils in a given situation is one of the greatest challenges which the teacher will face. This means that from time to time the teacher will not get things quite right. In such a situation you can play a vital role in ensuring that pupils in a group access learning which is both interesting and relevant to their learning needs. In Chapter 3 we examined the relationship between teaching and learning. In this chapter we will build upon those issues in order to further an understanding of how pupils may respond to a range of classroom teaching situations. In particular this chapter will focus upon the standards highlighted in the box below:

HLTA STANDARDS

1.1   Have high expectations of all pupils; respect their social, cultural, linguistic, religious and ethnic backgrounds; and are committed to raising their educational achievement.

1.2   Build and maintain successful relationships with pupils, treat them consistently, with respect and consideration, and are concerned for their development as learners.

2.3   They understand the aims, content, teaching strategies and intended outcomes for the lessons in which they are involved, andunderstand the place of these in the related teaching programme.

2.5   Know the key factors that can affect the way pupils learn.

2.9   Know a range of strategies to establish a purposeful learning environment and to promote good behaviour.

3.1.2   Working within a framework set by the teacher, they plan their role in lessons, including how they will provide feedback to pupils and colleagues on pupils' learning and behaviour.

3.2.2   Monitor pupils' responses to learning tasks and modify their approach accordingly.

3.2.3   Monitor pupils' participation and progress, providing feedback to teachers, and giving constructive support to pupils as they learn.

3.3.1   Using clearly structured teaching and learning activities, they interest and motivate pupils, and advance their learning.

3.3.3   Promote and support the inclusion of all pupils in the learning activities in which they are involved.

3.3.5   Advance pupils' learning in a range of classroom settings, including working with individuals, small groups and whole classes where the assigned teacher is not present.

3.3.8   Organise and manage safely the learning activities, the physical teaching space and resources for which they are given responsibility.

CHAPTER OBJECTIVES

By the end of this chapter you should:

● have an understanding of why teachers form different groups;

● appreciate a range of strategies for ensuring that pupils can participate in group work at a level appropriate to their needs and abilities;

● be aware of the importance of observing pupils in group situations in order to inform assessment and planning;

● build upon the work covered in Chapter 3 to see how teaching and learning styles may have an impact upon the formation and management of groups;

● be aware of environment factors, which may determine the success or failure of group work.

How and why do teachers use group work?

Before considering how and why teachers form particular groupings it is important that we draw a distinction between grouping and group work. Teachers may often group pupils together around a table and expect them to work independently at tasks in this situation. This 'grouping' of pupils does not require pupils to collaborate together on a task but, rather is, a locational matter of pupils sitting in close proximity working as individuals. 'Group work' demands that pupils co-operate together in learning, working together on tasks either under the direction and supervision of an adult, or independently. This requires that pupils demonstrate an ability to share materials, exchange ideas, respect the opinions of others and negotiate in order to undertake their work. Adults working with pupils in this situation need to be able to encourage collaboration while providing direction, checking understanding and progress, and sometimes acting as a catalyst for activity which pupils may not initiate alone. Managing group work effectively requires a sophisticated range of skills and can make a considerable difference in terms of pupils' achievement and learning.

Effective teachers use a range of strategies to ensure that all pupils have access to learning. During the course of a school day, pupils are likely to experience whole class teaching, group work, possibly some paired work and even some individual tuition. Each of these approaches is important in enabling the teacher to communicate information, assess understanding and help pupils to develop as effective team workers and individual learners. Much of what we do in society is managed in teams or groups and learning to function effectively in this situation is an important requirement of education. Learning to work co-operatively can enhance pupil self-esteem, build important classroom friendships and move pupils away from the dependency which can arise in some didactic teaching situations. Some researchers (Johnson, Johnson and Johnson-Holubec 1990, Spenciner and Putnam 1998) have emphasised the need for careful structuring of groups to provide a well-balanced set of learning experiences for pupils. This is particularly true where groups are of diverse need and ability. For some pupils group work can be an unsatisfactory experience where not well managed, particularly where this results in the marginalisation of individuals who feel left out from activities. It is crucial that careful attention is given to planning groups rather than simply expecting that pupils will co-operate and thereby learn.

Teachers group pupils in a variety of ways depending upon what is to be learned, the classroom situation and how they perceive that pupils will work together. These groups may be based upon a number of factors and may be described as:

- **Ability groups:** where all the pupils working together are of a similar ability and may work together on a task which requires a similar level of skills. This form of grouping may have advantages in some situations. For example, it may be used in a mathematics lesson where the teacher wishes a group of the most able pupils to work together on activities to extend their knowledge and understanding.

- **Mixed ability groups:** in which pupils of a wide range of needs and abilities work together on an activity. This can often provide an opportunity for the most able pupils to support those who are having some difficulties with learning. It provides pupils with learning difficulties with good learning role models and, where managed, can encourage the most able to further their understanding by explaining more difficult concepts to their peers.

- **Friendship groups:** can be effective because pupils who get on well together are likely to co-operate more readily. However, these groups often need to be carefully managed in order to keep pupils on task, and teachers also need to be aware of individuals who may not have friends in the class and can therefore feel excluded.

- **Interest groups:** may sometimes be formed where teachers are encouraging pupils to work on particular projects within a lesson, which demands a particular range of knowledge on the part of the pupils. For example a teacher may be working with pupils on the production of a class magazine in English lessons. Some pupils may be writing a section about the town football team, others might be describing the local carnival, while a further group might be reviewing a film recently shown at the local cinema. Such activity depends upon the prior experience and interest of the pupils and may therefore lead to groupings according to their interests.

PRACTICAL TASK

Take two days from your most recent week in school. By going through the timetable for these two days, how many of the above forms of group work can you identify?

- Can you see the reasons why the teacher grouped the pupils in these ways?

- Might they have been grouped in other ways?

Talk to the teacher(s) involved and ask them to explain why they grouped the pupils in the ways that they did.

The skills required for managing groups

Managing groups of pupils effectively makes considerable demands upon the teacher or teaching assistant. The ways in which groups are managed may depend upon a number of factors. These will include the size of the group, the abilities, behaviour and needs of the pupils within the group and the task to be undertaken. Bennett and Dunne (1995) suggest that most teachers in secondary schools form groups of four to six pupils when they are attempting to promote collaborative working. Similar numbers are usual in primary schools. You will observe that in any group work situation pupils are likely to adopt specific roles. Some will be dominant characters who want to lead, others may be content to follow, while some may be reluctant participants. Learning takes place when individuals learn to do something which they couldn't do before; this is certainly true in group work situations. As a professional teaching assistant you will need to observe the different roles which individuals play. Those who usually play a more passive role in group work situations need to be encouraged to take some leadership responsibility from time to time. However, this will only be achieved if they are confident with the task set for the group and when they are clear about your expectations.

***

Case study

Jayashree is a teaching assistant working in a middle school. Every Wednesday afternoon she works with Peter, who teaches geography to a year 7 group. This term the pupils have been considering environmental issues within the local area. The teacher has adopted a geographical inquiry approach with questions, which include: how the local area is changing, the impact of these changes and what the local residents feel about these changes. In today's lesson on how the land use around the school has changed and is continuing to be developed the pupils are going to examine old maps, current maps, photographs and statistical data in order to decide what their own response is to the changes that have taken place. One pupil, Nigel, is enthusiastic about geography but usually takes a passive role in group activities. Jayashree has noted that Nigel has very good knowledge of the local area and decides to encourage him to make use of his expertise in a greater leadership role. She suggests to the group that they need to identify a series of questions which they will later use in a survey of local residents based upon the materials provided by the teacher for this lesson. Making use of Nigel's knowledge, she appoints him as the co-ordinator of the group to provide information to the others and devise a plan of action to complete the task set by the teacher.

***

In the case study presented above, we can see how the teaching assistant has managed the group in order to ensure greater participation by an individual pupil. Without her support Nigel would have taken a more passive role and his learning experience would not have been so effectively enhanced. The decisions which Jayashree made in order to plan this group session, were based upon her good knowledge of Nigel, his needs and interests. She recognised that Nigel was enthusiastic about the subject and that he had a particular expertise, which was important to the successful outcome of the activity – namely a good knowledge of the locality around the school. However, without her intervention and careful planning, Nigel may still have played a passive role. Jayashree needed to define clearly the role which Nigel would play and ensure that the other members of the group realised what was expected both of him and themselves.

The teaching assistant in the case study made good use of her knowledge of pupil expertise. This can only be achieved when a teaching assistant gets to know pupils well and takes the time to reflect upon how they will react in different situations. All pupils come to school with a range of experiences and knowledge; having an appreciation of this can enable the teaching assistant to support pupils in making use of their expertise and by so doing enhance their self-esteem. There is no reason why, for example, a pupil with special educational needs who happens to have specific knowledge, should not be encouraged to take a prominent role in group work situations. For example, a pupil with learning difficulties who happens to be a member of the Sikh religion may have unique understanding which provides an opportunity to play a leading role during a group activity looking into religious festivals. This may have a positive impact upon the pupil's self-image and may also change the ways in which he is regarded by his peers.

Managing a range of abilities in group work situations

When working with mixed ability groups it is often a challenge to ensure that all pupils are fully involved and contributing at an appropriate level. Pollard and Tann (1987) pointed out that classes in schools vary considerably with regard to the ways in which they respect individuality and difference and that the behaviour of adults is critical in promoting positive attitudes and acceptance of others. Pupils are often acutely aware of their own individuality. In the case of pupils with special educational needs or those who are gifted or talented this may lead to them becoming withdrawn and reluctant to participate in group activity. Leyden (2002) has suggested that the most able pupils often demonstrate distinctive intellectual characteristics, which may include curiosity, initiative, attention to detail and independence. These are all traits, which we would wish to encourage in learners. However, they are also factors, which if not recognised and addressed, may lead to individuals becoming bored and restless in group work situations. Teaching assistants managing groups can play an essential role in ensuring that the most able pupils are adequately challenged in group work situations. Eyre (1997) suggests that in addition to ensuring that the work set for the able pupil is at an appropriate level, the teaching assistant may play a vital part in challenging the pupil with questions and discussion which extends their current knowledge and understanding. This, of course, requires that the teaching assistant enter the situation aware of the needs of the pupil and with a carefully constructed plan of how to challenge their learning. As a professional teaching assistant you will learn to recognise when some pupils need additional support quite quickly. Far more difficult to achieve is a recognition of when pupils need to be left alone in order to gain greater independence as learners. It is always helpful to take the time to reflect upon what went well in group work situations and how each individual pupil responded to the situation. The time to do this is not always available. However, if you develop a structured approach to assessing the effectiveness of group work, you will be far more effective in feeding back information to teachers about the effectiveness of various learning situations and about the performance of individual pupils.

The next task is designed to encourage you to identify the needs of individuals and to think about how they will be both supported and challenged in a group work situation.

PRACTICAL TASK

Identify a mixed ability group with whom you have worked recently. Fill in the chart below by considering what the overall learning objectives for the group activity were and how individual learning needs and strengths could be planned for in this activity. If you have an opportunity to do so, discuss your chart with the pupils who were involved in the activity. Are their perceptions the same as yours?

The first line of the chart (Elizabeth) has been provided as an example.

Date:			
Objectives for the group activity:			
PUPIL'S NAME	LEARNING STRENGTHS	INDIVIDUAL LEARNING OBJECTIVES	WHAT CAN I DO TO SUPPORT LEARNING?
Example: Elizabeth	Good reader Articulate Good general knowledge	To encourage her to look at different ways of solving a problem	Use of questioning to challenge her current knowledge

Observing learning in group work situations, recording and reporting to teachers

An important part of your task as a professional teaching assistant will be feeding back to teachers about what happens in the groups which you manage. The practical activity above was intended to help you to consider the needs of individual pupils and to identify how these might be addressed during group activity. You will be most effective in supporting teaching and learning when you have a systematic approach to observing what happens in the group work situation in order that you can record the responses of individual pupils and feed back information to teachers. Observing what is happening in a busy group work situation when you are responsible for the management of pupils and the organisation of activity is a daunting task. It is also one which requires that you are systematic and clear about the purposes of the observation and the information you want to obtain. Tilstone (1998) provides practical advice on this issue, suggesting that through careful observation and recording we can learn both *about* and *from* pupils. You need to be able to provide teachers with information about pupil performance, behaviours, understanding and collaboration in group work situations. At times it will be most profitable to focus upon specific individuals within a group. For example, a teacher may wish to know whether a particular pupil can generalise his mathematical learning into practical applications in a group activity, or if an individual pupil is able to cope working alongside others of greater ability. In order to provide this information you may well adopt a checklist similar to the one below.

Observation of group work activity

Pupil's name
What was the purpose of the activity for this pupil?
Was the purpose achieved?
What did the pupil do well?
What did the pupil find difficult?
What does the pupil need to practise?
How did the pupil interact with others in the group?

This is just one, fairly simple, example of the kind of checklist which may be of help in observing and recording what happens in a group work situation. It will, however, provide the kind of information that may be of value to the teacher. The information gathered may enable the teacher or yourself to plan for further action with the pupil concerned. It may also enable the teacher to make decisions about whether classroom groupings are appropriate or what changes might be necessary. It is useful to retain such records and to revisit them from time to time to see whether individual pupils have retained or refined their skills and to assist the teacher in making judgements about both the progress of the individual and the effectiveness of group work.

You might like to try designing your own checklists and to try them out in your own school situation.

Creating an environment for effective group work

There are, of course, a number of influences which may have an impact upon the success or failure of group work situations. Careful consideration about creating the correct climate and environment for groups can help prevent a lot of difficulties. It is always helpful to begin by thinking about the nature of the activity set for the group.

- Is it likely to be a noisy activity?
- Does it require a quiet atmosphere?
- What kind of space is needed?
- Does the activity need to be near to specific resources such as water or a computer?
- Will the activity be a particular distraction to others in the class?

These questions, and others like them, if considered in advance of the lesson, may assist in ensuring that the activity runs smoothly. When working with a group of pupils you will want to maintain control by having all of the pupils in a location, which is easy for you to manage. Similarly, this situation will be most comfortable if all of the facilities you need are in place and pupils do not have to spend time wandering around the room. Being prepared before the session is obviously a major help in ensuring that group work goes well. Think before hand about the environment in which you will be working, and be prepared to discuss this with the teacher. For example, if you are working on a task such as a mathematics problem which requires a quiet atmosphere in which pupils can concentrate, this may not be achieved if the rest of the class are involved in a noisy debate. Similarly, consider distractions which may take pupils off task during your group work session. If they are located next to a window with a view of builders working on installing new playground equipment outside, this might just prove to be more interesting than the activity you have planned for them! Can you position the pupils in such a way that they can concentrate upon what you are doing with them rather than looking out of the window?

Distraction can be a problem in any teaching situation but there is much that can be done to minimise this disruption. When managing a group activity make sure that the pupils have all of the equipment which is needed to complete the task, this will save them having to walk around the class or waiting around while others finish with a piece of apparatus. However, having too much clutter around can also lead to disruption with pupils fiddling with materials which are not required for the activity. Create the kind of working space which gives pupils room in which to operate, is not cluttered and does not have distracting irrelevant materials lying around.

Remember also that the pupils themselves are part of the learning environment. Think about where you seat pupils in order to avoid disruptive behaviours. How do individuals get along with each other? Try to avoid sitting pupils together who do not get along. Similarly, if there is a pupil in the group who often causes difficulties, be prepared to position yourself close to this pupil in order that you can keep watch on their behaviour and offer encouragement to stay on task. Thinking carefully about all of these issues can make the difference between a successful session and one which leaves both yourself and the learners in your care feeling frustrated and disappointed with the learning situation.

The effective management of group work is something which even experienced teachers often find difficult. As with other aspects of classroom management it will help to discuss the formation, management and effectiveness of groups with the teacher responsible for the management of the class. Group activity does not always go well and this may be for a variety of reasons including the appropriateness of the work set for the group, the time available, the working environment or the relationships between individuals in the group. While many teachers focus upon the work output of groups, it is essential that as a professional teaching assistant you are also able to concentrate upon matters of group formation and the creation of a good working climate. When effectively managed, group work can be rewarding for both teachers and learners. Adopting an organised approach to the management of group work should enable you to become proficient in establishing and working with a variety of groups.

Summary

Effective group work requires:

- Good knowledge of the pupils in the group.
- Careful planning of activities with attention to both group and individual objectives.
- Good record keeping based upon observation and understanding of intended learning outcomes.
- Efficient management of space and resources.
- Creation of a comfortable and effective learning environment.
- Time to feed back information to teachers.

References

Bennett, N and Dunne, E (1995) Managing groupwork, in Moon, B and Shelton-Mayes, A, *Teaching and learning in the secondary school*. London: Routledge.

Eyre, D (1997) *Able children in ordinary schools*. London: David Fulton.

Johnson, DW, Johnson, RT and Johnson-Holubec, E. (1990) *Circles of learning*. Minnesota: Interaction Book Company.

Leyden, S (2002) *Supporting the child of exceptional ability*. (3rd edn) London: David Fulton.

Pollard, A and Tann, S (1987) *Reflective teaching in the primary school*. London: Cassell.

Speciner, LJ and Putnam, JW (1998) Supporting young children's development through co-operative activities, in JW Putnam (ed.) *Co-operative learning and strategies for inclusion*. Baltimore: Paul Brookes.

Tilstone, C (1998) *Observing teaching and learning*. London: David Fulton.

Introduction

For many of us who went to school before a time when computers were in common educational use, information and communications technology (ICT) is a relatively new subject. It is true to say that there are still some professional colleagues in school who regard computers and the technology surrounding them as something for those who are clever or of a scientific disposition, yet ICT plays a part in all of our everyday lives. Whether it be going shopping where the goods we purchase are likely to be checked through a bar code reader and entered into a computerised till which automatically records levels of stock of that item, or through the use of a mobile telephone, a DVD player or a digital camera, we cannot escape the fact that ICT plays an important role in all of our lives. For this reason if none other, it is important that the pupils in our schools become familiar with the influences and uses of information technology in the societies in which they will live. If we additionally consider the ways in which ICT can be used to help both pupils and ourselves to learn, the ways in which it can be used to enhance the learning environment, and the many opportunities for making learning more exciting and interesting, then we can see why it is now regarded as an important factor within our education system. While computers may not have been a common feature of classrooms in the past, we should now expect that all pupils work in environments where the computer is taken for granted (Leask 2004). Primary schools provide the foundations of learning in ICT which should mean that pupils leave at the end of Key Stage 2 with the understanding and skills in use of ICT which enable them to become increasingly independent learners as they progress through their school lives (Ager 2003).

As a professional teaching assistant you will be expected to have a good understanding of the different ways in which computers and other technology may be used in your school. You should also gain confidence in the use of equipment and software, which can both enhance your own work and make life easier for you in your professional role. While you are unlikely to learn everything that ICT can do in a learning environment, your confidence and familiarity with systems which are in common use will help both pupils and teachers to feel supported in the classes in which you work.

One important consideration with regard to the use of ICT in education relates to equal opportunities. Many of the pupils with whom you come into contact will have access to computers and possibly other ICT at home. This will not be true of all. It is important when working with pupils that you do not make assumptions about their ability to access information at home from sources such as the internet. Similarly, because some pupils will be using computers regularly at home, they may have a greater understanding of how they operate and be confident in their use. Other pupils will need the most fundamental introductions in order to encourage them to use computers. You can play an important role in identifying levels of pupil confidence and competence and ensuring that this is effectively communicated to the teachers with whom you work. You have an equally important duty to ensure that those pupils who need extra support in order to access learning through ICT gain your attention when it is most needed.

In this chapter we consider how ICT is used in schools and is taught as a subject, how it is used to support other subjects, how it can be developed as a teaching aid and assist you personally as you further develop your skills as a professional teaching assistant. In particular the chapter will focus upon the standards highlighted in the box below:

HLTA STANDARDS

2.4 They know how to use ICT to advance pupils' learning, and can use common ICT tools for their own and pupils' benefit.

3.1.3 They contribute effectively to the selection and preparation of teaching resources that meet the diversity of pupils' needs and interests.

3.3.8 They organise and manage safely the learning activities, the physical teaching space and resources for which they are given responsibility.

CHAPTER OBJECTIVES

By the end of the chapter you should:

● have familiarised yourself with some of the hardware and software most commonly used in schools;

● have an appreciation of the ways in which ICT may be used to support and enhance the learning of pupils;

● be conversant with the ways in which you may use ICT to support your own work;

● recognise the potential opportunities provided by the internet, and have some appreciation of how this might be used safely.

A note on terminology

Some people are put off the use of information and communications technology by the technical language which is used by 'experts' who have devoted a considerable amount of time to become familiar with the details of the technology and functions of the computer. While it is helpful to develop an understanding of the most commonly used technical terms, it is not essential to acquire a detailed vocabulary in order to become effective in supporting learning through use of ICT. For those of you who are keen to take your learning in this area to a more advanced level there are many books that can help you. Within this chapter my concern is to assist you in a consideration of the use of ICT in classrooms rather than to provide a detailed technical understanding of the operations of computers and other hardware. For this reason we will restrict the use of technical vocabulary to those points which may be necessary to assist you in fulfilling your role as a professional teaching assistant. Two terms, which we do use throughout the chapter, are hardware and software. These have been used in the following way:

- **Hardware:** refers to equipment such as computers, digital cameras or interactive whiteboards which are directly used to provide access to means of communication, information retrieval or software which pupils may use in learning.

- **Software:** refers to those computer programmes (e.g. Clicker, Working with Symbols) which may be stored in a variety of formats (such as disk, or CD ROM) which contains information which needs to be accessed through appropriate hardware.

Becoming familiar with ICT in your school

It is only possible to gain confidence in ICT through familiarity with the hardware and software and its use. It is quite possible that there is a lot of ICT within the school with which you may seldom or in some cases never come into direct contact. It is most important that you begin by familiarising yourself with that equipment which is in regular use in the classes with which you have regular contact. In particular, there is likely to be hardware and software that is used by teachers and pupils as a normal part of everyday practice. If you are unfamiliar with equipment, you should not be afraid to ask someone to demonstrate this to you when they have the time. It can be both time-consuming and embarrassing to try to figure out how something works when trying to work with a group of pupils. Everyone has to learn how to use new resources, and your own understanding will be accelerated if someone who is confident with the equipment gives you an introduction to ICT. This need not necessarily be a teacher, who may be busy and have difficulty in finding the time. Often a keen pupil will enjoy demonstrating during lunchtime or break, how a program or piece of hardware works. By asking for such help you may not only be increasing your own knowledge and skills, but may also be reinforcing the learning of a pupil and raising their self-esteem.

PRACTICAL TASK

In order to familiarise yourself with ICT that is in regular use in a classroom in which you work, complete the following chart. After each lesson fill in the chart to indicate what hardware and software was used during the lesson. For some lessons there will probably be no use of ICT. Use the relevant boxes to indicate your own level of confidence (high, medium or low) in this ICT and at the end of the week discuss with a teacher those areas in which you feel the need for some training or support.

HARDWARE OR SOFTWARE BEING USED	LESSON IN WHICH IT WAS BEING USED	LEVEL OF PERSONAL CONFIDENCE
		High Medium Low
		High Medium Low
		High Medium Low
		High Medium Low
		High Medium Low
		High Medium Low

If you have low confidence in the use of any hardware or software which is in regular use, you should certainly seek some help to improve your own skills, knowledge and understanding. If you believe you have medium confidence, this might simply mean that you need more opportunity to work with the equipment or to practise alone at a quiet time.

Teaching ICT as a subject

In order to make effective use of ICT, pupils need to be taught how to access and gain confidence in the use of a range of hardware. The National Curriculum identifies ICT as a discrete subject, which has a clearly defined purpose:

> *Pupils use ICT tools to find, explore, analyse, exchange and present information responsibly, creatively and with discrimination. They learn how to employ ICT to enable rapid access to ideas and experiences from a wide range of people, communities and cultures.*
>
> (Department for Education and Employment 1999)

The above statement provides an indication of the kinds of skills and understanding which pupils are expected to acquire through the teaching of ICT, and highlights the ways in which you may be able to support learning. In the majority of primary schools, most learning about ICT and its use is incorporated into other subjects. For example, pupils may use the internet to find information about life in Roman Britain, they may take digital photographs during a field trip to illustrate features of a river valley as part of a geography project or they may use a desktop publishing package to produce a newspaper as part of their work in English. Whatever they are using ICT for, they will need to develop confidence and competence with respect to accessing and using hardware and software. The following case study demonstrates how one teaching assistant who was fairly confident in the use of ICT helped a group of pupils to develop their own ICT skills, and in so doing produced information which would assist others in the class.

Case study

Greg is a teaching assistant who works predominantly in a year 5 and 6 class in a junior school. In two weeks time the class will be going on a school visit to a local farm where they will be looking at, among other things, the ways in which the land is used and how and why the farmer makes decisions about how to manage the land. As part of this process the teacher wants pupils to be able to record the day using a digital camera. Greg is keen on using ICT and is familiar with the school's newly acquired digital cameras and how to transfer pictures from the camera to the computer and onto CDs. During a lesson last week Greg worked with a group of five pupils who were encouraged to become familiar with the new digital cameras. In the lesson they learned how to take pictures, how to transfer these to the computer and to use software which enabled them to edit and improve the quality of their pictures. Once they were confident in this process Greg split the group into two. Three pupils worked together to produce a PowerPoint presentation which described how to use the digital camera. The other two pupils produced a PowerPoint presentation on editing pictures.

During the next week's lesson the pupils used their PowerPoint presentations to demonstrate use of the digital cameras to their classmates. After this, all of the pupils practised with the cameras and transferred their pictures to the computer.

In this case study we can identify a number of important features. First, Greg was quite confident in the use of the digital cameras and had a good understanding of how to use PowerPoint. This was essential in enabling him to provide effective guidance to the pupils in his charge. Secondly, as with many activities using ICT, he was working with a small group of pupils which enabled all of them to have easy access to the limited hardware available. An important feature of this session is the encouragement which pupils were given to demonstrate their own learning. By producing PowerPoint presentations for use with their peers they had to consider their own understanding and how best to communicate this to others. Such an approach builds upon pupil understanding and enhances learning. This was not a discrete ICT lesson as such, being part of a geography lesson, but it did focus upon the development of ICT competence, thus enabling pupils to become more confident and effective in the use of the hardware and software.

Supporting learning in other subjects through ICT

ICT is being used increasingly by teachers in all subjects of the curriculum. The National Curriculum identifies four specific areas in which pupils need to develop their knowledge, skills and understanding, these being:

- finding things out;
- developing ideas and making things happen;
- exchanging and sharing information;
- reviewing, modifying and evaluating work as it progresses.

Pupils are afforded opportunities to address these four areas in a variety of ways and it is helpful for you to be able to distinguish these in order to ensure that you have sufficient knowledge and understanding to be able to support pupils effectively. If we take these four areas and consider what they mean in terms of using ICT we must do so first in relation to the skills which pupils are intended to develop. For example, finding things out should not be seen just with regard to ICT. Pupils need to be able to gain information from a wide range of sources, including books, video or DVD materials, magazines or newspapers and through talking to people. ICT can provide an additional source of information, possibly through use of CD ROM or the internet, but will not necessarily always be the most appropriate source of information. Issues such as ease of access, the suitability of materials, level of information, and accuracy will always need to be considered when encouraging pupils to seek information. However, the use of ICT may prove particularly useful either to supplement information from other sources or to provide a stimulus for further investigation. For example, if you are asked to support pupils in finding information about the life and works of a famous author as part of an English project, you should begin by familiarising yourself with a range of potential sources. Pupils will make most effective use of any source of information when they are encouraged to find answers to carefully phrased questions. This will ensure two things. First, it will encourage pupils to remain clearly focused on the information required. Secondly, it will save them the time of searching through a source only to find that the necessary information is unavailable. Pupils will be greatly aided in their learning and will not become frustrated if you follow a logical sequence of events.

- Familiarise yourself with the information, e.g. website or CD ROM which you intend that pupils should use.
- Provide specific questions to enable pupils to gather information and ensure that the answers can be found on the website or CD ROM to be used.
- Encourage pupils to make use of a range of media and not to expect that they can always find their information from one source.
- When pupils provide you with the information, check the source from which this was obtained and talk to the pupils about the advantages or disadvantages of using this media.

Quite rightly, some adults have expressed concerns with regards to the safety of the internet and the ability to control pupil access. Schools will have safety systems in place which ensure that pupils cannot gain access to websites which contain materials of an unpleasant or dangerous nature. However, when working with pupils using the internet, you have a responsibility to exercise some control over the materials which they access. This relates not only to content which may be unpleasant or dangerous but also you need to ensure that the reading level of materials is at a suitable level, that the information is accurate and the materials accessible.

Pupils can be encouraged to develop their ideas through use of ICT in many ways. For example, in art lessons pupils may be encouraged to examine the work of an artist and from this to generate their own design. The advantages which a computer may offer is in enabling pupils to save their design, make different versions of this by changing colour or shape and reviewing their progress by revisiting earlier saved versions. Similarly, pupils may use word processing in order to develop drafts of stories or reports and can be encouraged to modify or change these after they have acquired new information or ideas. In such ways they are enabled to improve their own performance and learning.

It is said that we live in the communications age. Certainly schools today are often equipped with sophisticated equipment which enables both staff and pupils to exchange information in a variety of ways. Pupils are increasingly using e-mail in order to request information from other sources. At another level they are now able, through the use of graphics pages, digital images and desktop publishing to produce high quality posters or other display materials which enable them to share their ideas with others. Some schools have developed class newsletters and many today have school websites to which pupils contribute their own ideas and information and on which they display their work.

Individual teachers have their own views about how ICT may be most effectively used in the classroom. To some extent this is related to their own experiences and confidence, it may also be related to the availability and suitability of software and the range of ICT resources available in schools. The availability of hardware such as interactive whiteboards, digital cameras and the internet has greatly increased in recent years, but is still dependent upon the allocation of financial resources. This inevitably means that while some classrooms are well equipped others are less so, and also recognises that expensive apparatus often needs to be shared and timetabled. As a professional teaching assistant you need to familiarise yourself with the different ways in which teachers are making use of ICT and to identify those areas of the curriculum in which it is regularly used. Once you have done this, you should be able to develop your own knowledge of the hardware and software which is in use and ensure your own confidence with this. You may also be able to consider how those subjects where ICT is not currently used may benefit from its use.

Providing access to learning

There may be pupils in the classes with whom you work who are enabled to access the curriculum through the use of ICT. Computers and other forms of ICT are being increasingly used to support the education of pupils with special educational needs. Much of the available software used in schools today has accessibility facilities. This may simply mean the ability to change the size or colour of font or background to make reading easier for some pupils or in some instances will include a voice accessibility system for pupils unable to use a keyboard. The use of adapted keyboards, for example with enlarged keys or switching devices, may be essential for some pupils with a physical disability. Similarly, schools are making increasing use of symbol software to provide access for pupils who have little or no literacy. Pupils who, for physical reasons, are unable to write, may have their own laptops or word processors, and pupils unable to talk may have a voice simulator. Clearly, if you are required to support such pupils you will need to become familiar with the specific equipment or software allocated to the pupil. There are a number of helpful texts, which may provide information about aspects of supporting pupils with special educational needs through the use of ICT (Detheridge and Stevens 2001, Singleton, Ross and Flavell 2003). The SENCO in your school may also have access to useful information should you need to work with such equipment.

Using ICT for your own professional benefit

As well as providing pupils with opportunities for learning, ICT may have an important role in enabling you to become more effective in your day-to-day working. ICT may assist you in keeping your records, preparing work for pupils, preparing presentations or writing reports. Some schools will have long established systems for recording, keeping records or sharing information which require use of ICT and clearly you will need to become familiar with these. ICT provides many potential advantages for your work. For example, you will identify sessions which you teach, possibly to whole class groups or smaller groups, which come around every year. By storing your lesson plan, worksheets or presentation on a computer disk, CD or memory stick, you will be able to call on this in the future, make necessary amendments for updating and potentially save considerable time in preparation. Proficiency in the use of the internet or other information devices such as CD ROMs will enable you to make use of varied and interesting materials in your preparation of lessons, and learning how to transfer pictures into documents or for the production of PowerPoint presentations will enhance your teaching materials.

PRACTICAL TASK

Consider a session which you will be teaching during the next few weeks and answer the following questions.

- Do I have all of the information and knowledge I need to teach this session?

- If not, can I find out more through use of the internet?

- Can I identify an opportunity to use ICT during the session?

- Why would I use the ICT – what benefits will it have for pupils?

- What skills, knowledge and understanding do pupils need in order to use this ICT?

- Will I need to teach specific skills in order that pupils can use the ICT?

- What benefits will the use of ICT have for my teaching?.

We should not assume that all lessons benefit from an ICT content. Asking these questions should help you to remain focused on the issue of ICT providing benefits to both the learner and the teacher.

The pace at which ICT continues to develop is considerable. Keeping up to date with the latest technology and the ways in which it may be used in schools is a challenging task. Not everyone will become an 'expert' in the development of ICT but all who work in classrooms need to update their training in this area on a regular basis. Your school will have an ICT co-ordinator who should be able to advise you in this area.

Summary

Effective use of ICT requires that you:

- develop your own level of confidence and competence;
- become familiar with the hardware and software commonly used in your school;
- recognise the different needs and abilities of pupils with respect to ICT use;
- endeavour to keep abreast of new innovations coming into the school.

References

Ager, R (2003) *Information and communications technology in primary schools*. London: David Fulton.

Department for Education and Employment (1999) *Information and communication technology: The National Curriculum for England*. London: DfEE/QCA.

Detheridge, T and Stevens, C (2001) Information and communication technology, in Carpenter, B, Ashdown, R and Bovair, K (eds) *Enabling access*. London: David Fulton.

Leask, M (2004) Using ICT in the classroom and for administration, in Capel, S, Heilbronn, R and Turner, T (eds) *Starting to teach in the secondary school*. London: Routledge Falmer.

Singleton, L, Ross, I and Flavell, L (2003) *Access to ICT*. London: David Fulton.

6. Creating equal opportunities

Introduction

Pupils are likely to learn most effectively when they feel secure and comfortable in their schools. Treating pupils with respect, providing them with a school ethos which is supportive, and ensuring that their personal beliefs and cultural background is recognised and celebrated, is an important factor in enabling them to access an appropriate education. In the UK we are fortunate in living in a multi-cultural and diverse society. This provides a unique opportunity for pupils to learn together in a way which enables them to understand and appreciate a variety of cultures and beliefs, to share in a celebration of diversity and to learn to respect the views of others from the community in which they will live. Unfortunately, for a significant number of pupils in the past, schools were not the welcoming and supportive places, which we would hope that they now aspire to be.

As a professional teaching assistant there is much that you can do to support your school in the promotion of equal opportunities. Your own personal professional conduct provides an important starting point for ensuring that pupils learn to respect the rights of others and to recognise the benefits of living in a diverse community. In this chapter we will examine some of the ways in which you can provide this support and consider some of the issues which arise in schools. In particular the chapter will focus upon the standards highlighted in the box below.

HLTA STANDARDS

1.1 They have high expectations of all pupils; respect their social, cultural, linguistic, religious and ethnic backgrounds; and are committed to raising their educational achievement.

2.5 They know the key factors that can affect the way pupils learn.

3.3.2 They communicate effectively and sensitively with pupils to support their learning.

3.3.7 They recognise and respond effectively to equal opportunities issues as they arise, including by challenging stereotyped views, and by challenging bullying or harassment, following relevant policies and procedures.

Legislative framework

Schools have a responsibility to comply with laws which promote equal opportunities. This is an issue which is given a high priority at LEA and national government level and has generally been addressed in schools through the development of policies which aim to ensure that pupils are not discriminated against. As a professional teaching assistant you should familiarise yourself with school policies and consider how these are implemented in the school. You should also reflect upon your own responsibilities in ensuring that you provide support for these policies, thereby affording protection to pupils in the school who may otherwise be vulnerable.

Equal opportunities in the UK are legislated through a number of Acts of Parliament and other statutes to which schools must pay attention. These include the following:

Sex Discrimination Act 1975

While this Act is aimed mainly at employers it does have a section which deals specifically with education which makes it unlawful to discriminate between boys and girls. It has been influential in encouraging greater equality of opportunity in the curriculum. For example, it would now be unlawful to deny girls the opportunity to study courses in woodwork or engineering, or to prohibit boys from taking a course in cookery.

Race Relations Act 1976

This Act makes it unlawful to discriminate against individuals or treat them less favourably on racial grounds. The Act recognises individuals in respect of their race, colour, nationality (including their citizenship) but not their religion. This Act was amended in 2000 by the Race Relations (Amendment Act) which was implemented following the Stephen Lawrence Inquiry. This Act emphasises the duty of public bodies, including schools, actively to promote racial equality.

The Disability Discrimination Act (DDA) 1995 and the Special Educational Needs and Disability Act (SENDA) 2001

This legislation places a duty upon schools not to treat pupils less favourably because of a special educational need or disability. It calls upon schools to make reasonable adjustments to ensure that such pupils are not disadvantaged.

Removing Barriers to Achievement 2004

This document outlines the ways in which schools can ensure that they create a more inclusive learning environment and promote positive actions to support pupils from disadvantaged or marginalised groups and in particular those with special educational needs.

The Children Act 2004

This Act encourages greater co-ordination of planning between all agencies supporting children. It has four central strands which encourage:

- early intervention;
- improving accountability and co-ordination of children's services;
- improving support for parents and carers;
- a childcare workforce strategy.

The importance of high expectations

The expectations which adults have with regards to the potential of individual pupils may be based upon a number of factors. Where teachers are provided with detailed assessment information about pupils' past academic performances, this may have a positive impact in enabling them to ensure that they plan work at an appropriate level to meet individual learning needs. However, there have been many occasions when the expectations of pupils have been based upon misinformation or the stereotyping which has plagued the lives of many groups within our societies. Within the guidance provided to Ofsted inspectors is a section which asks questions such as: *Is the curriculum socially inclusive by ensuring equality of access and opportunities for all pupils?*

This reinforces a statement from the National Curriculum:

> *When planning teachers should set high expectations and provide opportunities for all pupils to achieve, including boys and girls, pupils with special educational needs, pupils with disabilities, pupils from all social and cultural backgrounds, pupils of different ethnic groups including travellers, refugees and asylum seekers, and those from diverse linguistic backgrounds. Teachers need to be aware that pupils bring to school different experiences, interests and strengths which will influence the way in which they learn.*
>
> (DfEE 1999, p31.)

Schools have for many years been urged to give a high priority to the development of equal opportunities policies and to the consideration of how they create a learning environment which recognises differences of culture, faith and social background in the school population. However, as Bayley and Paterson (1997) indicated, while most schools would claim to have developed equal opportunities policies, there may be times when its application remains somewhat superficial. The principles of equal opportunities are founded upon basic human rights. These rights assert that it is wrong to discriminate against individuals on grounds of their colour, race, religion, sexuality, disability, social class or nationality. In 1989 the United Nations General Assembly unanimously adopted the Convention on the Rights of the Child. This important document not only affords protection to children, but also asserts the responsibilities of adults to ensure that the rights of children are upheld. For those of us working in education there is an additional responsibility which comes with our duty of care to those children who are directly within our charge.

Children need good role models if they are to learn how to treat others with respect. We cannot always guarantee that they will have these role models at home and this increases the responsibility of schools to provide clear indicators to all pupils with regard to what is acceptable or unacceptable behaviour. If pupils see you behaving in a manner which they interpret as being unfair to individuals within the school, they may assume that this is acceptable and infers a right for them to behave in a discriminatory manner. You are therefore under an obligation to provide an example to all pupils of fairness and respect, which you can then expect to see replicated in the pupils with whom you work.

Unfortunately, there are many young people from minority or marginalised groups living within our society who report negative experiences of schooling. Some of these experiences relate directly to the low expectations of teachers. Kerry Noble, a young lady with cerebral palsy recalling some of her school experiences writes:

> *When teachers set me a piece of work, I began to realise that certain teachers would praise my work regardless of the amount of effort I had made or the quality of the work produced. As a consequence of this I became lazy and did not make as much effort as I should. I suspect that had I been able-bodied they would have had a different attitude.*

(Noble 2003, p60)

Myrie (1995) writing about the experiences of black Afro-Caribbean students in the English education system describes similar experiences of low expectation and stereotyping of pupils simply on the grounds of their colour and cultural background. Further experiences of low expectations have been recorded from the gypsy traveller community (Derrington and Kendall 2004) and those for whom English is an additional language (Helavaara-Robertson and Hill 2001).

We should, of course, question where our expectations of pupils have their origin. It is, for example, quite possible that those teachers who had low expectations of Kerry Noble's educational abilities (incidentally Kerry has subsequently obtained a degree), had previously not had experience of teaching a pupil with a physical disability. Indeed, their low expectations may have been, in part, based upon their wanting to show kindness to Kerry rather than through some intentional plan to inhibit her learning. Similarly, when teachers are confronted by a pupil who speaks little or no English, this is likely to provide a challenge to teaching which may be a new experience for that teacher. In the case of the students studied by Myrie, we can see findings that concur with a national picture of underachievement by pupils, and especially boys, from the Afro-Caribbean community. The stereotyped image of this population has for long been one of a group of pupils who have a negative approach to learning. As with other stereotypes, the persistence of myths and misinformation can have a damaging effect upon the achievements of a whole group of pupils. While teachers may have had only limited experience of teaching pupils from minority groups, this does not constitute a good reason for having low expectations.

As a professional teaching assistant, you can take a number of steps to overcome some of the obstacles to learning faced by pupils from minority groups. First of all you can increase your own knowledge about the backgrounds, beliefs and needs of the pupils with whom you work. Beginning from a principle of not relying on hearsay and anecdote but finding out as much as you can about those aspects of a pupils' life which may have an impact upon their learning will give you insights which may prove beneficial to individual pupils and the school as a whole. Listening to the advice of those professional colleagues who have specific expertise, such as the special educational needs co-ordinator or a teacher from the multi-cultural education service will often prove helpful in enabling you to understand more about the pupils with whom you are expected to work.

PRACTICAL TASK

Consider the following scenario.

Michaela, a 9-year-old refugee from Albania, has just joined the class in which you work as a Teaching Assistant. She has only a limited understanding of English and knows no one else in the school. She appears very quiet and, while other children in the class are curious about her and want to be friendly, she seems confused and lacks the confidence to join in most lessons. The class teacher has asked you to spend some time getting to know her and to support her in lessons.

- How will you begin to form a relationship with Michaela?

- What information might help you to support her effectively?

- Where might you gain this information?

- What kind of things might you do to encourage Michaela to join in with other pupils?

- What do you think might make Michaela feel most welcome and part of the class?

When you have considered these questions discuss them with a colleague in your school.

Do you have the same ideas, views and perceptions?

Curriculum access and equal opportunities

When the National Curriculum was revised in 1999 a renewed emphasis upon the teaching of citizenship was perceived as providing an opportunity for schools to ensure that issues related to equal opportunities received greater attention. This shift in emphasis was received positively by many teachers who have been concerned that the balance of the school curriculum was greatly skewed towards academic outcomes, with insufficient attention being given to the social and moral development of pupils. However, the promotion of equal opportunities cannot be achieved through the teaching of citizenship alone. The principles, which underpin equality of opportunity, need to be fully embedded in all aspects of the curriculum.

The National Curriculum has identified three principles for inclusion which are critical to achieving equal opportunities within the curriculum, These are:

- setting suitable learning challenges;
- responding to pupils' diverse learning needs;
- overcoming potential barriers to learning and assessment for individual pupils and groups of pupils.

These statements are made in recognition of the fact that classes are seldom made up of homogeneous groups of pupils who will all respond to the same teaching approaches, but rather that teachers and other colleagues will need to plan lessons which take into account a wide range of needs and abilities. Pupils need to engage with the curriculum and should feel that it is directly relevant to them. Responding to diverse learning needs means that teachers and teaching assistants need to take care in selecting teaching materials and adopting approaches which recognise the individuality of pupils. Schools in recent years have become much more adept in selecting resources which reflect the cultural make-up of our society. The National Curriculum urges schools to ensure that pupils have access to, for example, stories and music from a range of cultures. Most English schools today do make a point of celebrating festivals from other faiths such as Diwali or Eid and some make arrangements for visits to places of worship such as synagogues or mosques. In so doing, they assist pupils in recognising the importance of respecting and valuing the beliefs of others. As a professional teaching assistant you can support this process by learning more about the faith and beliefs of others in order to be able to discuss ideas with pupils in an informed manner.

Pupils with disabilities or for whom English is an additional language may encounter several obstacles to accessing the curriculum. Those with disabilities may need adaptations to equipment or materials and may require additional practical support from yourself. There are a number of important principles to bear in mind when working with such pupils. First, remember that the pupils themselves are most knowledgeable about what supports or inhibits their learning. Before intervening with help, ask them about what support they feel they need. Try to be discreet when providing support; many pupils will feel self-conscious and possibly embarrassed if the help which you provide to them singles them out as being different from others. Seek advice from the class teacher and other experts who are familiar with the needs of the pupil. In the case of a pupil with a disability, the school special educational needs co-ordinator or a member of the LEA support services may be able to provide advice. In all cases, the pupil's parents will have knowledge and expertise which is crucial to the provision of support and can ensure curriculum access.

Pupils who have limited understanding of English present both challenges and opportunities to the teacher. When working with these children it is important to begin with a recognition that their personal language experiences are likely to be as rich, and possibly even richer, than those of the other pupils in the class. The majority of pupils who enter schools with limited English do so because of a previous lack of exposure to the language. However, these pupils are likely to be proficient in use of their first language and in some instances may also be competent in two or more languages. Consider the case study below.

Case study

Hanif joined a year 3 class at St David's Primary School at the beginning of this term. On entering school it was apparent that Hanif had a few words of English. He was able to say 'good morning' and knew the words 'yes' and 'no' and could use 'please' and 'thank you'. Other than this his knowledge of English was limited. His first language, and that spoken most frequently at Hanif's home, is Pahari but he is also familiar with Urdu.

Hanif has settled quickly into class and has made a number of friends. Once a week he is visited by a support worker from the county multi-cultural service whose first language is Urdu. She provides advice to the teacher and talks to Hanif about how he is getting on in his new school. She has worked with the class teacher to identify some of the key vocabulary which will be used in some of this term's work and has provided a set of vocabulary cards, written in both English and Urdu for the teacher to use.

The teacher has asked Angela, the teaching assistant in the class, to spend time with Hanif assisting him in learning the vocabulary provided and helping him with pronunciation. Angela has identified a group of Hanif's

> *friends in the class and has decided that it might help if, in addition to Hanif learning the English vocabulary, he acts as a teacher and teaches his friends the equivalent vocabulary in Urdu. The pupils get together at the beginning of each morning and during some lunchtimes to play a game using the vocabulary cards.*
>
> *After a couple of weeks, Angela and the class teacher notice that Hanif's English vocabulary has extended well beyond the materials provided on the vocabulary cards and that he has developed a wider social vocabulary. Many of his friends have also learned how to greet Hanif in Urdu and have also acquired language other than that presented on the teaching materials.*

In this situation, the teaching assistant has played an important role in helping Hanif to gain confidence in school. She has demonstrated respect for his own language skills and has encouraged him to build positive relationships with others in the class. She has also made effective use of a simple range of resources provided by a colleague and recognised that Hanif's peers could enhance his learning opportunities if they were also involved in this process. The fact that other pupils in the class have learned some Urdu may be seen as incidental to the original purpose of the activities provided. However, this might also be regarded as an important 'by product' of the approach as it has enhanced their understanding of Hanif's cultural and linguistic background. The professional approach adopted by the teaching assistant in this situation has been essential in enabling Hanif to feel welcome in the school and to recognise that he will be able to succeed in learning alongside his peers.

Teaching assistants need to work in a systematic way when supporting pupils such as Hanif. There are a number of factors which can assist pupils in gaining proficiency in English to which you should adhere. These include:

- showing respect for the language and culture of the pupil;
- encouraging and appreciating the use of the pupil's home language to support learning;
- accepting non-verbal responses where appropriate;
- modelling early writing skills – such as movement from left to right;
- using additional visual materials to enable pupils to gain understanding of matters being discussed;
- repeating instructions and keeping these short;
- reading to pupils and demonstrating pronunciation and intonation;
- correcting the pupil's pronunciation in a positive manner through modelling;
- allowing pupils sufficient time to think before demanding an answer to questions.

Many schools have become more aware of the relatively straightforward steps that they can take to promote an appreciation of the diversity within our communities. When visiting schools it is now common to see displays which represent a range of faiths, cultures, abilities and languages. However, simply mounting such displays will have minimal impact upon the promotion of equal opportunities unless effective use is made of them.

Case study

Following the Olympic Games in Athens, pupils in a year 6 class have produced a display showing the achievements of British athletes. This display includes representation of successful British athletes from the paralympics. As part of the term's work in science, the class teacher has been teaching the pupils about energy efficiency. As part of this work the pupils consider the design of wheelchairs used by the disabled athletes. They then compare the athletic qualities and requirements of runners with those of the wheelchair athletes.

This example demonstrates how a display which demonstrates the achievements of both able-bodied and disabled athletes can be used effectively to show that the achievements of the wheelchair athletes is comparable to that of their non-disabled counterparts.

PRACTICAL TASK

Examine the displays around your school. To what extent do they celebrate diversity? Consider how you might use some of the work displayed in a session which you might lead with a group of pupils.

Awareness of bullying

All adults working in schools need to be aware of bullying. When considering the needs of pupils who come from minority groups there is a particular need for vigilance. Bullying is unacceptable wherever or whenever it occurs and schools must take appropriate actions to deal with incidents whenever they occur. Research does indicate that those pupils who come from minority groups are often more vulnerable and likely to be bullied (O'Moore and Hillery 1992, Rutter 2001). As a professional teaching assistant you need to be aware of the potential for bullying and to know what actions you should take if it is encountered.

In 1999 the DfEE issued a circular which stated that:

The emotional distress caused by bullying in whatever form, be it racial, or as a result of a child's appearance, behaviour or special educational needs, or related to sexual orientation – can prejudice school achievement, lead to lateness or truancy and, in extreme cases, end with suicide. A third of girls and a quarter of boys are at some time afraid of going to school because of bullying. Bullying is usually part of a pattern of behaviour rather than an isolated incident. Pupils should be encouraged to report any bullying to staff or to older pupils they can trust. Low report rates should not of themselves be taken as proof that bullying is not occurring

(DfEE 1999b)

Pupils who are the victims of bullying need support, yet recent research (O'Moore and Minton 2003) indicates that the majority of pupils are very reluctant to report incidents to adults. Pupils need to be given advice on bullying and what to do when it occurs. You will obviously need to work closely with teaching staff and be aware of school policy when dealing with any matters related to bullying. However, as an adult who will have a close relationship with pupils, you should not only be aware of the possible signs of bullying but should also be clear about the actions which you must take for the protection of pupils. If a pupil comes to you and says that he or she is being bullied you must:

- ensure that you are conversant with school policy;
- make time to listen to the pupil – somewhere where the pupil feels safe and that they will not be overheard;
- be cautious about making promises, e.g. if the pupil says they do not want you to tell anyone else this will be impossible if you think the pupil is at risk;
- record carefully what the pupil has told you;
- report what you know to a teacher – in some schools there may be a designated teacher who deals with such incidents;
- reassure the pupil that you will be taking action, let them know what you intend doing, and that they can come to you again if they have further concerns.

You have a clear duty if you have any concerns that a pupil may be the victim of bullying, to report this to a teacher. You will not be expected to deal with incidents of bullying alone. It is important that you are aware of possible signs, which you may detect in school, which *could* be an indication of bullying. These include:

- unexplained bruises, scratches or cuts;
- torn or damaged clothes or belongings;
- reporting non-specific pains, headaches or stomach ache;
- fear of walking to or from school;
- deterioration in school work;
- lost dinner money;
- significant changes of behaviour;

- becoming withdrawn;
- stammering;
- unexpected mood change, irritability and temper outbursts;
- appearing distressed, tearful or upset;
- loss of weight.

All of these can be indicators of bullying, though they may be symptomatic of other problems. Whatever their cause, if you notice any of the above in relation to a pupil with whom you work, you should report your concerns. It is far better to express your worries and for them to be proven unfounded, than not to report them and have a pupil suffer.

The promotion of equal opportunities is an important part of the process of education for all in schools. It should not be viewed as separate from other aspects of school management and organisation but should be implicit in everything that happens in the school. The example, which you set to others and the ways in which you interact with pupils, can make a significant difference to the development of a more equitable society. The principles discussed in this chapter should underpin all of the work which you do and should be considered in relation to the contents of every other chapter in this book.

Summary

- The promotion of equal opportunities is fundamental to the working of all schools.
- You should act in a way that can be seen to provide a positive role model for all within the school community.
- By learning more about the cultural, religious, and linguistic diversity of pupils within schools, you will be better able to promote positive approaches for the development of equal opportunities.
- You should be vigilant in respect of harassment or potential bullying of pupils at all times.
- Equal opportunities should be implicit in all aspects of teaching and learning and throughout the school curriculum.

References

Bayley, R and Paterson, G (1997) Putting principles into practice, in Cole M, Hill, D and Shan, S (eds) *Promoting equality in primary schools*. London: Cassell.

Department for Education and Employment (1999a) *The National Curriculum*. London: DfEE.

Department for Education and Employment (1999b) Circular 10/99 *Social inclusion, pupils support*. London: DfEE.

Derrington, C and Kendall, S (2004) *Gypsy traveller students in secondary schools: culture, identity and achievement*. Stoke-on-Trent: Trentham.

Helavaara-Robertson, L and Hill, R (2001) Excluded voices: educational exclusion and inclusion, in Hill, D and Cole, M (eds) *Schooling and equality: fact, concept and policy*. London: Kogan Page.

Myrie, D (1995) Experiences of black students, in Potts, P, Armstrong, F and Masterton, M (eds) *Equality and diversity in education. (Vol. 1) Learning, teaching and managing in schools*. Routledge: London.

Noble, K (2003) Personal reflection on experiences of special and mainstream education, in Shevlin, M and Rose, R (eds) *Encouraging voices*. Dublin: National Disability Authority.

O'Moore, AM and Hillery, B (1992) What do teachers need to know? in Elliot, M (ed) *Bullying: a practical guide to coping for schools*. London: Longman.

O'Moore, AM and Minton, S (2003) The hidden voice of bullying, in Shevlin, M and Rose, R (eds) *Encouraging voices*. Dublin: National Disability Authority.

Rutter, J (2001) *Supporting refugee children in 21st century Britain*. Stoke-on-Trent: Trentham Books.

United Nations (1989) *The convention on the rights of the child*. New York: United Nations General Assembly.

www.multiverse.ac.uk

7. Creating inclusive classrooms

Introduction

Teachers are responsible for ensuring that the learning needs of all pupils in their class are addressed. There are many factors which might have an influence upon the learning successes of pupils, and teachers need to develop a wide range of teaching approaches and classroom management skills in order to provide appropriate learning experiences for all pupils. In 1997 the government issued *Excellence for All Children* (DfEE 1997). In this Green Paper they outlined a vision for the development of schools which would address the needs of a diverse population and include pupils who have previously attended special schools or have in other ways been marginalised within mainstream classrooms. This was followed by practical advice given in *Removing Barriers to Achievement: The Government's Strategy for SEN* (2004) a document with which you should become familiar as it discusses how schools may move towards the creation of more inclusive learning environments. The notion of inclusion, while often ill-defined has become important in establishing a commitment to classrooms which are equitable and in which teachers and teaching assistants can work together in partnership to provide for a diverse population of learners.

Educational inclusion has often been narrowly interpreted as the ability of schools to address the learning of pupils with special educational needs. This is an inappropriate way of defining inclusion, which should be seen as the development of a school to be able to address the needs of all pupils within the community which it serves. Florian (1998) suggests that we should regard inclusion as a *philosophy of education that promotes the education of all pupils in mainstream schools* (p13). However, she also argues that simply adopting such a philosophy will not ensure that all pupils have access to learning and that schools need to revise their ideas about and approaches to teaching in order to create classrooms in which all pupils succeed. Other writers have further developed Florian's views. Booth and Ainscow (1998) have endorsed a view that inclusion, having been largely focused upon pupils with special educational needs, has limited our understanding of the need to develop schools which address the needs of all pupils. This narrow approach to addressing inclusion is in danger of denying the importance of other needs which are experienced by pupils from a wide range of marginalised groups. Pupils from ethnic minority groups, those for whom English is an additional language, and others who come from communities which are socially and economically disadvantaged may all experience difficulties in accessing learning unless positive steps are taken to develop classrooms and teaching approaches which recognise individual needs. Rose and Shevlin (2004) have demonstrated that the educational experiences of pupils from these marginalised groups often follow a similar pattern of discrimination and failure which could be avoided with careful planning and a commitment to greater inclusion. Farrell and Balshaw (2002) suggest that the role of the teaching assistant may be critical in enabling teachers to create inclusive classrooms and to ensure that pupils who might otherwise be denied opportunities become effective learners.

While recognising that the principles of inclusion must apply to all pupils, and that in the past some have been excluded by a school system which has failed to address a wide range of needs and abilities, it is clear that legislation which has aimed to promote inclusion has focused upon those described as having special educational needs. Within the previous chapter we examined some of the wider aspects of promoting equal opportunities in schools. The principles outlined in that chapter are essential in ensuring that all pupils are provided with access to an education which recognises and celebrates a diversity of culture, language, needs and abilities. This chapter gives consideration to how teachers and teaching assistants are required to respond to the legislation governing special educational needs in order to promote inclusive classrooms. It will also offer comment on how the principles of effective classroom practice may have a positive impact upon a diverse school population. In particular, this chapter will focus upon the standards highlighted in the box below:

HLTA STANDARDS

1.1 Have high expectations of all pupils; respect their social, cultural, linguistic, religious and ethnic backgrounds; and are committed to raising their educational achievement.

1.2 Build and maintain successful relationships with pupils, treat them consistently, with respect and consideration, and are concerned for their development as learners.

2.5 Know the key factors that can affect the way pupils learn.

2.8 Know the legal definition of Special Educational Needs (SEN) and are familiar with the guidance about meeting SEN given in the SEN Code of Practice.

3.1.3 Contribute effectively to the selection and preparation of teaching resources that meet the diversity of pupils' needs and interests

3.2.2 Monitor pupils' responses to learning tasks and modify their approach accordingly.

3.2.3 Monitor pupils' participation and progress, providing feedback to teachers, and giving constructive support to pupils as they learn.

3.3.1 Using clearly structured teaching and learning activities, they interest and motivate pupils, and advance their learning.

3.3.2 Communicate effectively and sensitively with pupils to support their learning.

3.3.3 Promote and support the inclusion of all pupils in the learning activities in which they are involved.

3.3.7 Recognise and respond effectively to equal opportunities issues as they arise, including by challenging stereotyped views, and by challenging bullying or harassment, following relevant policies and procedures.

CHAPTER OBJECTIVES

By the end of this chapter you should:

● be familiar with the special educational needs policy for your school;

● know the ways in which your school responds to the requirements of the *Special Educational Needs Code of Practice* (2001);

● be aware of the factors which may influence and impede learning in some pupils;

● have considered approaches to supporting pupils of diverse needs in a range of teaching situations;

● be aware of the importance of monitoring the progress of pupils who have difficulties with accessing learning.

The Education Act 1996 defined special educational needs by stating that:

Children have special educational needs if they have a learning difficulty which calls for special education to be made for them.

Children have a learning difficulty if they:

a) *have a significantly greater difficulty in learning than the majority of children of the same age; or*

b) *have a disability which prevents or hinders them from making use of educational facilities of a kind generally provided for children of the same age in schools within the area of the local education authority;*

c) *are under compulsory school age and fall within the definition of a) or b) above or would do so if special educational provision was not made for them.*

Children must not be regarded as having a learning difficulty solely because the language or form of language of their home is different from the language in which they will be taught.

(Education Act 1996, Section 312)

This Act was important not only in establishing a working definition of special educational needs but also in setting out principles which should encourage high expectations of all pupils regardless of needs or ability. Low expectations of pupils on the basis of a label attached to them has been a major inhibiting factor for many pupils described as having special educational needs. There is always a danger that a pupil with a label such as Down's syndrome or dyslexic will be subjected to stereotyped images which lead to false assumptions about learning on the part of the teacher or teaching assistant. There are many people thus labelled who have proven themselves to be successful learners and whose achievements are equal to others who have not been subjected to such labels. Jarvis, Iantaffi and Sinka (2003) have collected the opinions of deaf pupils about their experiences of mainstream schooling. By reading the views of these pupils, we are able to see the fine line between approaches from adults which are genuinely supportive of learning and others which, while well meaning are in fact discriminatory and humiliating. One 8-year-old describes how adults 'act strangely' when they know about the pupil's deafness. They talk in an overdramatic way, emphasising the syllables of words. This pupil states: *Please don't do that. I prefer it if you talk normally. I'm not Stupid* (p210).

The adults who 'act strangely' are in all probability doing so because they believe they are being helpful and hope to enable the pupil to understand their meaning more readily. However, it is clear from this pupil's response that such behaviour is condescending and may have an inhibiting effect upon learning. Adults need to listen to pupils and take guidance from them on how they wish to be approached and what can assist them in accessing learning or, in the example given, communication. It is quite clear that some of the adults working with the pupil referred to here have low expectations of this pupil's ability to communicate based upon a limited understanding of deafness.

While the example cited above refers to a pupil who is deaf, the principles discussed might equally be applied to any pupil from a minority group. Labelling is often a precursor to stereotypical views of pupils. The importance of overcoming such stereotyping and adopting high expectations of all pupils is a theme which recurs throughout the literature. Melzak and Warner (1992) found that refugee children from Eritrea on entering schools in Sweden referred to teachers who had clear and high expectations as being those with whom they liked to work. Gillborn and Gipps (1996) found that expectations of pupils from Asian communities in the UK were often low with adults anticipating difficulties with language resulting from their interpretation of cultural factors. This was particularly true with regards to girls from the Asian community. It is evident from much of the research into the inclusion of pupils from minority groups that negative attitudes and low expectations can be the first barrier to successful inclusion. As a professional teaching assistant you can do much to ensure that all pupils benefit from a proper understanding of their learning needs. This begins by getting to know pupils well, and by listening to their views and experiences and trying to see their perspectives on the ways in which they feel most able to learn. Engendering positive attitudes is an essential part of beginning a successful learning process and must be founded upon mutual trust and high expectation.

The Special Educational Needs Code of Practice

In 1994 the government issued a *Code of Practice on the Identification and Assessment of Special Educational Needs*. This was subsequently updated in 2001 with a new *Special Educational Needs Code of Practice*. This important document provides a framework whereby schools must take action to support any pupil who is experiencing difficulties with learning and may consequently be identified as having a special educational need. It is essential that as a professional teaching assistant you become fully conversant with this document.

The *Code of Practice* adopts a graduated approach to the assessment and planning for pupils with special educational needs. It does this through the implementation of stages of assessment and the identification of actions to be adopted by schools through *School Action* and *School Action Plus* (or in the case of pupils in the early years this is *Early Years Action* and *Early Years Action Plus*) both of which require schools to put in place procedures to ensure that the needs of individual pupils are addressed. In a minority of cases pupils may be given a *statement of special educational needs*, which is a statutory document recognising that the pupil's needs cannot be met using the resources normally available within the school, and setting out how provision to meet the pupil's needs will be assured.

Teaching assistants often find themselves assigned to work with pupils described as having special educational needs and therefore need to be aware of the requirements of the *Code of Practice* and the impact this has upon the pupils in a class. The *Code of Practice* is informed by the following set of principles.

- A child with special educational needs should have their needs met.
- The special educational needs of a child will normally be met in mainstream schools or early education settings.
- The views of the child should be sought and taken into account.
- Parents have a vital role to play in supporting their child's education.
- Children with special educational needs should be offered full access to a broad, balanced and relevant education, including an appropriate curriculum for the Foundation Stage and the National Curriculum.

These principles need to be adhered to by the school and as a professional teaching assistant you may play a critical role in supporting this process. Early identification of any difficulties which a pupil may be experiencing can help to ensure that appropriate support is put into place and in some instances may enable the pupil to overcome barriers to learning and ensure that progress in learning is maintained. As a teaching assistant you will often get to know pupils very well and your observations on their behaviour, any difficulties which they experience in learning or anxieties which they express, can provide critical information in the early stages of pupil assessment. Indeed, your vigilance as a teaching assistant may, in some instances, be essential in ensuring that a pupil receives the support required to enable them to receive the resources they need and to learn efficiently.

The *Code of Practice* suggests that the key for a school to take action is a recognition that the current rate of progress being made by the pupil is inadequate. Teachers are required to conduct regular assessments of pupils and to provide evidence of their progress. This will enable them to measure progress against that of their peers and against national expectations. As a teaching assistant you can assist this process by informing the teacher of any concerns which you may have and by keeping your own records of how pupils respond to activities or tasks which you manage. The term 'adequate progress' is complex, particularly when considering that we should not expect all pupils to progress at the same pace. However, the *Code of Practice* does provide helpful advice on this matter. Paragraph 5.42 on page 52 of the *Code of Practice* states that:

> *Adequate progress can be defined in a number of ways. It might, for instance, be progress which:*
>
> - *closes the attainment gap between the child and their peers;*
> - *prevents the attainment gap growing wider;*
> - *is similar to that of peers starting from the same assessment baseline, but less than that of the majority of peers;*
> - *matches or betters the child's previous rate of progress;*
> - *ensures access to the full curriculum;*
> - *demonstrates an improvement in self-help, social or personal skills;*
> - *demonstrates improvements in the child's behaviour.*

Where a pupil is not making adequate progress, the teacher will normally engage in a conversation with the school's special educational needs co-ordinator (SENCO). If through the observations and assessments made, and following discussion with the SENCO, it is believed that the pupil will not learn unless interventions are made which are *additional to* or *different from* those which the teacher normally provides in class, then there may be a decision made to proceed to *School Action*. This means that plans will be made to introduce specific interventions to support the pupil in their learning. This may involve the development of a personalised programme for the pupil and often, teaching assistants play a major role in the delivery of this. The teacher remains responsible for the planning, assessment and monitoring of any programme put into place. At this stage it may also be decided that there is a need, with the consent of the parents, to involve professionals from other agencies, and again the teaching assistant may play a crucial role in gathering and providing evidence for these professional colleagues. (*See* Chapter 2 for further discussion of effective working in this situation.)

Identify a pupil for whom School Action has been implemented. Make a list of the difficulties which this pupil experiences with learning. Examine the teacher's short- and medium-term plans and see what actions have been put into place to support this pupil's learning. Consider why the teacher is taking these actions and how they may assist the pupil in becoming a more effective learner. Discuss this with the teacher and ask how the progress which the pupil is making is being monitored and recorded.

The strategies to be used to assist a pupil in making progress should be contained within an Individual Education Plan (IEP). This plan, which focuses specifically upon the needs of the individual pupil, needs to be made available to and understood by all who work with the individual concerned. The *Code of Practice* requires that the IEP should include:

- the short-term targets set for or by the child;
- the teaching strategies to be used;
- the provision to be put in place;
- when the plan is to be reviewed;
- success and/or exit criteria;
- outcomes (to be recorded when IEP is reviewed).

(*Code of Practice*, para. 5.50, p54)

If the pupil continues to make little or no progress, despite the efforts of the school through School Action, then the school may decide to move to *School Action Plus*. At this stage the school will request additional support from other agencies which may include, among others, an educational psychologist, a speech therapist, or a social worker. These professional colleagues may be asked to conduct more detailed assessments or may give input to the development of specific programmes or to the pupil's IEP. Again, the *Code of Practice* is fairly explicit in what might trigger School Action Plus, suggesting that this may be when a pupil:

- continues to make little or no progress in specific areas over a long period;
- continues working at National Curriculum levels substantially below that expected of children of similar age;
- continues to have difficulties in developing literacy and mathematics skills;
- has emotional and behavioural difficulties which substantially and regularly interfere with the child's own learning or that of the class group, despite having an individualised behaviour management programme;

- has sensory or physical needs, and requires additional specialist equipment or regular advice or visits by a specialist service;
- has ongoing communication or interaction difficulties that impede the development of social relationships and cause substantial barriers to learning.

(*Code of Practice*, para. 5.56, p55)

When a school implements School Action Plus, the intensity of activity surrounding a pupil is likely to increase. The pupil is likely to be aware of the concerns being expressed about their progress and may also feel some pressure from anxious parents or carers at home. As a professional teaching assistant, you will want to give the pupil as much support as you can, while also continuing to collate information and share your ideas with professional colleagues. In some instances it may be possible that a pupil will share their anxieties with you, particularly if they have a positive relationship with you and work with you on a regular basis. Teaching assistants can often play a vital role in offering pupils positive feedback with regard to their learning and thus provide the assurance which they seek.

In some cases, it will be necessary for schools to seek statutory assessment of a pupil which may result in a *Statement of Special Educational Needs* being issued. This will only happen after a school has gone through the necessary procedures at *School Action* and *School Action Plus*. When this has happened and the school still has concerns about a pupil, evidence may be collected and presented to the LEA who will consider whether a statutory assessment, which may lead to a *Statement of Special Educational Needs*, is appropriate. When a statement is issued it may result in the allocation of additional resources to support the pupil in school. This may include additional support time to be provided by a teaching assistant. In some cases the *Statement of Special Educational Needs* may recommend transfer to another school, possibly a special school, which has specialist provision to provide for the needs of the individual pupil.

Throughout this process, the progress of a pupil will need to be carefully monitored and regularly reviewed. The *Code of Practice* requires that IEPs are reviewed at least twice a year. However, many schools do this termly. For pupils with a *Statement of Special Educational Needs* there must be an annual review of the statement. This procedure should assess the pupil's progress towards established learning targets and should also review the provision made for the pupil. The annual review will be attended by the class teacher, by representatives of other agencies involved with the pupil, by parents or carers and, in most cases, by the pupil. Teaching assistants can play an important role in preparing pupils for their annual review as in the case study presented below.

Case study

Elizabeth is a teaching assistant working in the English Department of a large comprehensive school. Three times a week she supports Carl, a year 9 pupil who has been diagnosed as having dyslexia and who also has some social, emotional and behavioural problems. He has considerable difficulties with concentrating in lessons. Carl has a Statement of Special Educational Needs. He has difficulties with reading and finds spelling particularly difficult. In some English lessons Elizabeth works with Carl individually, helping him to keep on task with his work and encouraging him to check his own work and improve his accuracy. In three weeks time it will be Carl's annual review and Elizabeth has been given some extra time with him to support him through this process.

Carl is a little apprehensive about attending his annual review and Elizabeth has been trying to reassure him by talking to him about the progress which he has made and by emphasising the positive things which he has done since his last review. In order that he can demonstrate these aspects of his learning, Elizabeth is helping Carl to make a pictorial calendar, which highlights some of the activities and successes of the past year. Carl will be able to show this at his review without having to do too much reading. He has chosen photographs of some of the school events in which he has been involved, including a picture of the school football team for which he has played, and of a fund raising day for a local children's charity.

When they have finished making the calendar, Elizabeth will help Carl to rehearse what he wants to say about this at the annual review. The school has agreed that Elizabeth will attend the review with Carl in order to prompt him as necessary and to provide support.

In this case study Elizabeth plays a crucial role in enabling Carl to make a contribution to his own annual review. This could not be achieved unless she had a good relationship with him and also had a good understanding of his learning needs, the targets set for him and the ways in which he might be able to overcome his difficulties in taking part in the review. The same principles as those described here could equally be applied to supporting a pupil for whom English is an additional language through any formal assessment process.

The *Code of Practice* is the most important document governing the management of pupils with special educational needs and as a professional teaching assistant you should endeavour to become familiar with its content. You will also need to be conversant with the school's special educational needs policy and the documentation related to any pupils with special educational needs with whom you work.

Working in individual teaching situations

The withdrawal of pupils from the main class group to provide additional support, while common practice, is fraught with difficulties. There is a particular danger that pupils who are dealt with in this way may become ever more conscious of the fact that they are being treated differently and that this may have a negative impact upon their self-esteem. Similarly, there are dangers that pupils who are withdrawn will miss important learning opportunities which are afforded to others. The choice to withdraw a pupil needs to be carefully considered. While the decision to do so will rest with the teacher, if you find yourself working in this situation you will need to be aware of the importance of ensuring that the pupil is supported in a way that protects their self-esteem and enables them to see this form of working as advantageous. Much can be achieved by showing the individual pupil how the work that you do with them in a withdrawn situation may enable them to perform better when back in class. Teaching which is isolated from the main purpose of the class is likely to be limited in its impact and value.

It is, of course, quite possible to give effective support to an individual during the lesson within the classroom and alongside peers. This is a preferable way of supporting individual pupils and provides more opportunities for the pupil to interact with other members of the class. Providing support to individual pupils can be effective. However, it is important not to create dependency and to enable the individual to have time to work independently or with peers. Pupils can sometimes feel pressured if they have an adult working with them all of the time. Remember that your role is to support learning, not to do the pupil's work and not to inhibit interaction with the class.

When supporting an individual learner, whether this is a pupil with special educational needs, one for whom English is an additional language or any other pupil, certain principles may be applied.

- Be clear about what the teacher expects the pupil to achieve.
- Be aware of what parts of an activity the pupil may find difficult.
- Be aware of the pupil's previous learning in relation to the task set.
- Be well organised with all of the resources required.
- Think about how you will structure the session and how long you will spend on each task.
- Consider what you will assess. How will you know what the pupil has learned?
- Be prepared to offer constructive comments which help the pupil to reflect upon their own learning.
- Offer praise, which helps the pupil to gain in confidence.
- Be prepared to feed back to the teacher.

Individual teaching sessions should have a distinct pattern. Start by going over old ground, giving the pupil an opportunity to have early success in the lesson and thus gain confidence. If you can give the pupil something to do which you know they can achieve early in the session, you are likely to help them to feel confident before tackling more difficult tasks. However, be aware that learning occurs when the pupil can do something that they couldn't do before. Once the pupil has gained confidence through an initial task give them something more challenging to do. This means that you will need to know the pupil well in order to select the materials you will use during the session. Selection of materials is not simply a matter of knowing the resources, it is also about understanding when to introduce them and doing so in a way which will help the pupil to gain in confidence. When introducing new materials talk this through carefully with the pupil. Ensure that the pupil knows what is expected and be prepared to rehearse an activity several times before expecting the pupil to work alone.

When working with an individual, overdependency can be a problem. Pupils will often be able to do something with support but they need to be able to generalise this activity to other situations and to be able to work independently. When planning for individual teaching sessions always consider how you may be able to encourage the pupil to transfer learning to other situations. Give the pupil some time to work alone and be careful always to explain what you expect of the pupil.

Having stated that it is important to begin individual sessions by giving pupils work with which they can succeed, so is it necessary to finish on a similar high note. At the end of a session try to enable the pupil to finish by doing something well. In this way they will feel that they have accomplished something and will be looking forward to the next time they work with you. This may, in some instances, mean giving a simpler task at the end of the individual teaching session. This is perfectly acceptable, as you don't want the pupil to leave the session feeling that they have failed.

PRACTICAL TASK

Use the following format to plan a session for an individual pupil. The boxes provided should contain the following information.

- **Intended outcomes:** What is the purpose of the session, what do you hope that the pupil might learn?

- **Previous learning:** What can the pupil already do in relation to the activities planned?

- **Possible difficulties:** What might the pupil find hard and how might you help him/her with this?

- **Resources:** What resources and materials will you use?

- **Warm up activity:** What will you do at the start of the session in order to ensure that the pupil gains early success?

- **Main activity:** What will you be doing to encourage new learning?

- **Wind down activity:** How will you finish the session on a high note?

- **Assessment:** How will you know what the pupil has achieved? How will you record this achievement? What will you report to the teacher?

Date:
Intended outcomes:
Previous learning:
Possible difficulties:
Resources:
Warm up activity:
Main activity:
Wind down activity:
Assessment:

Pupils from minority groups, those with special educational needs and others who may be perceived as 'different' by their peers for whatever reason, often face challenges in the classroom based upon ignorance and prejudice. All pupils are entitled to an education that recognises their individuality and addresses their needs. As a professional teaching assistant you have a responsibility to provide support to pupils and to challenge negative views or stereotypes which are potentially damaging to the learning opportunities of pupils. In this chapter we have provided a brief overview of how you can provide practical classroom support for pupils who may be marginalised. Clearly this is a complex subject and one which you may need to study in greater depth. Elsewhere in this book we have considered issues of equal opportunities, learning and teaching styles, the management of groups and managing behaviour, all of which relate closely to the issues discussed in this chapter. In other books in The Professional Teaching Assistant series, the issues discussed here are explored in further detail. Most teaching assistants spend a significant amount of their time working with pupils who challenge conventional learning approaches and it is likely to be of considerable benefit if you take the time to study this area more fully so as to provide the maximum support to all pupils.

Summary

Inclusive classrooms are those where:

- All pupils are valued and opportunities are provided for them to participate fully in learning.
- The *Special Educational Needs Code of Practice* is adhered to in a way which is supportive of pupils, parents or carers, and school staff.
- Consideration is given to how individual pupil needs are addressed in the classroom.
- Good communication between teachers, teaching assistants and other colleagues is maintained.

References

Booth, T and Ainscow, M (eds) (1998) *From them to us*. London: Routledge.

Department for Education (1994) *Code of practice on the identification and assessment of special educational needs*. London: DfE.

Department for Education and Employment (1997) *Excellence for all children*. London: The Stationery Office.

Department for Education and Employment (1996) *Education Act*. London: DfEE.

Department for Education and Skills (2001) *Special educational needs code of practice*. London: DfES.

Department for Education and Skills (2004) *Removing Barriers to Achievement: The Government's Strategy for SEN*. London: DfES.

Farrell, P and Balshaw, M (2002) Can teaching assistants make special education inclusive? in Farrell, P and Ainscow, M (eds) *Making special education inclusive*. London: David Fulton.

Florian, L (1998) Inclusive practice: what, why and how? in Tilstone, C, Florian, L and Rose, R (eds) *Promoting inclusive practice*. London: Routledge.

Gillborn, D and Gipps, C (1996) *Recent research on the education of ethnic minority pupils*. London: HMSO.

Jarvis, J, Iantaffi, A and Sinka, I (2003) Inclusion in mainstream classrooms: experiences of deaf pupils, in Nind, M, Rix., J, Sheehy, K and Simmons, K (eds) *Inclusive education: diverse perspectives*. London: David Fulton.

Melzak, S and Warner, R (1992) *Integrating refugee children in schools*. London: Minority Rights Group.

Rose, R and Shevlin, M (2004) Encouraging voices: listening to young people who have been marginalised. *Support for Learning* 19 (4) 155–161.

8. Supporting processes of assessment

Introduction

Teachers are required regularly to assess pupils' performance, attainment, achievements and, where necessary, their behaviour. As a professional teaching assistant you have a critical role to play in assisting teachers in the performance of this important duty. Assessment takes many forms. Some is formal and is, in some instances, conducted so that schools comply with statutory requirements to gather information comparing progress against national standards. Other assessments are informal and are based upon the observations of teachers and teaching assistants in relation to often subtle changes possibly in respect of the performance of a pupil or their behaviour. Teachers use assessment information in order to plan their work, to gauge the effectiveness of teaching approaches or the success of resources and materials. The information which they gather may be used to make changes to teaching schemes of work, to inform the next stage of development in an IEP for a particular pupil or to report the progress which a child is making in a specific area of learning to their parents.

The proportion of time which teachers spend in assessment is considerable. This reflects both the importance which is attached to the process and the increased demands made by successive governments for schools to provide detailed information about academic performance. The pressure upon teachers to provide detailed and accurate assessment information is considerable and therefore the support which you provide to them in this process will be greatly appreciated. In this chapter we will consider the statutory requirements for assessment and examine the ways in which you, as a professional teaching assistant, may play a role in assisting with the collation and management of assessment information. Within this chapter we will address the following standards.

HLTA STANDARDS

3.1.2   Working within a framework set by the teacher, they plan their role in lessons including how they will provide feedback to pupils and colleagues on pupils' learning and behaviour.

3.2.1   They are able to support teachers in evaluating pupils' progress through a range of assessment activities.

3.2.2   They monitor pupils' responses to learning tasks and modify their approach accordingly.

3.2.3   They monitor pupils' participation and progress, providing feedback to teachers, and giving constructive support to pupils as they learn.

3.2.4   To contribute to maintaining and analysing records of pupils' progress.

The statutory basis of assessment

Much of the formal assessment conducted in schools relates to the requirements of the National Curriculum. Schools are required to publish the results of statutory assessments conducted for pupils at the ages of 7, 11 and 14. These statutory assessments measure the attainment of pupils and are compared with those of their peers across the country. The information gathered must be made available to the school's governing body and the Secretary of State for Education and must be published in the school's prospectus and in the annual report of the governing body. You will be familiar with these assessments, if only because of the amount of attention which they receive annually in the media. At Key Stage 1 an assessment using national tests must be made in mathematics and English (currently being reviewed). At Key Stages 2 and 3 there are national tests in English, mathematics and science. At each of these Key Stages a Teacher Assessment must be made in English, mathematics and science and at Key Stage 3 this is extended to embrace all Foundation subjects.

For staff working in early years settings and working within the foundation curriculum the use of Foundation Stage Profile and the accompanying assessment procedures is seen to be the most appropriate way to proceed. This system has replaced earlier baseline procedures and encourages dialogue between professionals and parents or carers in making accurate assessments of where pupils are in respect of a series of assessment scales. As a professional teaching assistant, if you are working with early years pupils you will need to be familiar with the six areas of learning and the assessment scales associated with these. Your confidence in relation to the assessment scales will enable you to use these for observations of pupils and to assist teachers who are required to maintain a profile for each individual pupil.

Teachers are obliged to keep records on every pupil, which includes records of academic and other achievements, skills and abilities and the progress which they make in school. These must be updated every year and must be transferred when a pupil changes school. Written reports to parents must be provided annually. This report must contain information about the pupil's progress in all subjects and activities studied as part of the school curriculum.

Information must also be provided on pupil attendance and performance in all National Curriculum Assessments along with national comparative data. For pupils with special educational needs there is a further requirement to conduct assessments and maintain records in line with the *Special Educational Needs Code of Practice* (DfES 2001). This will include records relating progress made to targets set as part of an IEP or, in some instances, an individual behaviour programme. (See Chapter 7 for a more detailed discussion of the *Special Educational Needs Code of Practice* (2001).) Your school will have many documents related to assessment, which ensure that statutory requirements are met and with which you should become familiar. Some schools have appointed assessment co-ordinators who should be able to help you and provide you with advice regarding the requirements in your school.

The nature and language of assessment

Assessment is usually seen to have two important functions within school, these being described as summative and formative.

Summative assessment

Summative assessment is conducted to identify the progress which pupils have made at the conclusion of a piece of work and their attainments and achievements against previously defined standards or criteria. This form of assessment might include standardised test results or assessments built into a scheme of work to judge the progress made at the end of a period of study.

Formative assessment

Formative assessment makes judgements about the progress pupils have made in respect of work which is currently being carried out with an intention of informing teachers and pupils about how their work may be modified improved or changed. This might include comments made on a piece of work, or a pupil's self-assessment of how they might improve a piece of work.

You may well hear other terms used in relation to assessment including:

- **Normative assessment:** where a pupil is assessed against an agreed norm;
- **Diagnostic assessment:** to ascertain strengths and weaknesses in respect of specific areas of development or learning;
- **Ipsative assessment:** where pupils are assessed to gauge progress in direct relation to previous learning.

However, most teachers are particularly concerned with summative and formative assessments and you are more likely to hear about these other forms of assessment from other professionals who may be involved with pupils, for example educational psychologists or speech therapists.

Schools will use a range of approaches to assess pupils. These may include standardised tests which measure factors such as pupils' reading age or spelling age against the norms for their peer group. They are also likely to use less formalised approaches such as observations of pupil behaviour in class or testing against learning objectives established in lesson plans or schemes of work in order to ensure that learning been achieved and that pupils have developed appropriate knowledge skills and understanding. It is generally accepted that all schools need to develop a range of approaches which are specifically matched to purpose in order to provide the breadth of information which teachers need in order to plan and deliver the curriculum successfully (Gipps 1993, Tilstone and Layton 2004). It is also accepted that teachers need to be clear about what they are assessing and why.

Some terms you will hear in respect of what is being assessed may seem similar but there are distinct differences of which you need to be aware. These include:

- progress;
- attainment;
- achievement.

Each of these three terms has a distinctly different meaning. Attainment relates to the ability of a pupil in a particular area of learning. For example, if a pupil is described as having reached level 4 in mathematics, this refers to the level of learning that the child has attained. In other words this is the level of his ability in mathematics. This is different from achievement, which refers to what a child has gained over a period of time and relates more closely to the nature of progress. It is also true to say that most formal assessment in schools is concerned with attainment against pre-set criteria and standards and that less attention is given to reporting pupil achievements and progress. This is best illustrated through the following case study.

This case study illustrates a number of important points with regards to the language of assessment. At the beginning of the year a standardised test is used to measure Michael's level of attainment. It indicates quite clearly that he is not reaching the level which would normally be expected of pupils of his age. Throughout the year Sue regularly assesses Michael in order to check how he is doing and to be sure of the effectiveness of the teaching materials being used. This is a formative process which provides both Sue and the class teacher with information enabling them to modify teaching approaches and materials. At the end of the year the standardised test is administered again as a form of summative assessment. The findings from this assessment reveal that Michael's reading attainment is still beneath his chronological age. However, he has made remarkable progress of 13 months advancement of reading age over a 10-month period. This is a notable achievement by Michael. Indeed, it could be that Michael's achievement in reading this year is better than that of any other pupil in the class despite the fact that his attainment is beneath that of his peers.

Case study

Michael is a 7-year-old pupil who attends his local primary school. He has some difficulties with learning, particularly in the area of English. He appears to have problems with following some verbal instructions and has considerable difficulty with reading and writing. At the beginning of the academic year Michael is assessed using a standard reading test, which records his reading age as 5.6 although his chronological age is 7.2. With the support of the LEA special educational needs support service, Michael's class teacher has written a programme of activities to support his reading. This is based upon Michael's interest in the local football team and appears to motivate him to want to read. The programme is carried out by Sue, the teaching assistant assigned to his class. Michael is regularly re-assessed by Sue throughout the teaching process in order to gauge both the success of the programme and to measure his progress. Sue reports on her findings about Michael's progress to the class teacher and maintains careful records. Where necessary she revisits work which he finds difficult or modifies materials to better address his needs.

At the end of the year when Michael is re-tested using the same standardised test it is found that his reading age has progressed over 10 months from 5.6 to 6.7; in other words progress of 13 months over a 10-month period.

These are important points for you to bear in mind. If the school simply reports reading ages at the end of the year, it will be clear that Michael is still behind most of his peers in his reading ability. It is therefore essential that achievement and progress are also celebrated and acknowledged. If Michael and his parents or carers are able to see the excellent progress which he has made, it is likely to raise his self-esteem and encourage him to continue working hard at his reading. If all that is reported is his attainment, then his parents or carers will be less pleased. Of course, the same positive effect will be felt with regard to the confidence and self-esteem of Michael's class teacher and of Sue who has worked so hard to help Michael make this significant progress.

Why do we assess pupils?

Pupils may be assessed for a number of reasons, which may include gaining a greater understanding of:

- what they have learned;
- their level of skills in a particular task or area;
- what they know and understand;

- the pace at which they are learning;
- their attitudes and opinions;
- how they learn best;
- what they need to learn next;
- the progress they have made over a period of time;
- their learning strengths and weaknesses;
- the effectiveness of teaching approaches or resources.

At various times teachers may focus upon any one of the above through formal assessment, but they will tend to keep all of these reasons for assessment in mind throughout their teaching and constantly be assessing in a less formal manner. You can assist the teacher by being aware of these assessment purposes and making note of your own observations of pupils' learning.

It is through accurate assessment information that teachers can ensure that the teaching approaches which they are using are effective in supporting the learning of all pupils. Experienced teachers gain an instinct for when a lesson is going well and pupils are learning effectively. However, instinct alone is not sufficient to enable teachers to judge accurately what is happening in class or in the lives of individual pupils. More formal assessment will often begin when a teacher has concerns or feelings about the progress, or lack of this, being made by individuals or groups of pupils. As a professional teaching assistant you can play an important role in identifying areas of concern or, in some instances, particularly good progress being made by pupils which warrants further investigation. As a teaching assistant you will probably observe things happening in class or with individuals which teachers miss. This is not because the teacher is less effective in their work but may be because you work more closely with an individual or group of pupils for certain activities or at particular times of the week. Your communication with the teacher is essential in identifying areas, which may be in need of further investigation or verification. Returning to the case study presented above, it appears that the class teacher had great confidence in Sue's ability to manage and monitor the teaching programme written for Michael. Sue was involved in regular assessment of Michael's progress and was able to communicate this regularly to the teacher. At the end of a period of teaching the class teacher implemented a more formal assessment through a reading test, which verified Sue's belief that Michael was making good progress. If we look at the list of purposes of assessment above, we can see that Sue is monitoring several of these every time she works with Michael. By keeping careful records of what happens in her sessions she is able to share this vital information with the class teacher. This kind of teamwork is very important in classrooms where teachers and teaching assistants work together as a team.

PRACTICAL ACTIVITY

Over the course of a week in class, identify as many different forms of assessment as you can. Most of this will be informal assessment of how pupils are progressing. You may also see formal assessment, for example spelling or maths tests. On the chart below enter the following information.

● What assessment took place?

● Was it formal or informal?

● How was the assessment information recorded?

● How was the information used?

● Who conducted the assessment?

When you have completed your chart ask the class teacher to take some time to discuss what you have found. She or he may be able to tell you about other assessments they have been using and will be able to discuss how assessments may be used.

WHAT ASSESSMENT TOOK PLACE?	FORMAL OR INFORMAL?	RECORDING METHOD	HOW WAS INFORMATION USED?	WHO ASSESSED?

Some important principles

There are some important principles which must be respected if assessment is going to be both effective and fair. Wherever possible, assessment should be an integral part of the teaching process rather than an add-on to it. Some pupils feel anxious when they know that they are going to be tested or assessed and may not perform so well under these circumstances. The more that assessment can be built into lessons as a standard feature the better it is likely to be received by pupils. In many instances the assessment process can be made enjoyable and even appear as part of a game. For example, the teacher who has been teaching pupils about using a ruler for measuring may devise an assessment whereby pupils are asked to design a car or a boat which must have certain dimensions which they must measure accurately. The activity can be made fun by getting the pupils to share their ideas and talk to the class about the design. This does not preclude the teacher from then examining the pupils' work to find out how accurate they are in their measuring.

There are equal opportunities associated with assessment and it is important that pupils are not put at a disadvantage. If you have a pupil in your group for whom English is an additional language and who is having difficulties with spoken and written English, you may have to use adapted assessment materials for some purposes. If they receive the same written test as other pupils, they may be put at a disadvantage and you may not in fact be assessing the same skills as you are for other pupils. Be aware of pupils with special educational needs who may require, for example, enlarged text or use of a word processor, or the provision of extra time in order to complete a test. They may be able to do as well as other pupils if the right conditions are put into place for them. The pupils themselves will usually be able to tell you what they need in order to access the assessment. All pupils benefit from a variety of assessment approaches. Bear in mind that some respond better to visual materials than others, while others prefer an auditory approach. The ways in which assessments are designed may give some pupils advantages over others. Adopting a variety of approaches will overcome this difficulty.

One-off assessments are often of limited use. That which a pupil may do with confidence today may be forgotten next week. Re-assessment is an important principle to which effective teachers adhere. A pupil may well have learned the fundamentals of long division last year, but if they have not practised this for some time they may need to be reminded of the essential principles. An assessment at the beginning of this process will provide useful information about what pupils have retained and how much needs to be revised.

Much informal assessment is based upon questioning of pupils to check on learning, understanding and retention. This is an important role, which as a professional teaching assistant you can fulfil. When working with pupils either individually, in small groups or as a whole class you should be able to gauge their understanding by the use of well phrased questions. Questioning in assessment is generally used to:

● find out what pupils know, understand and can do;
● analyse their responses and the questions, which they in turn ask;
● discover pupil misunderstandings or misconceptions;
● verify your perceptions of pupil performance.

Of course, questioning of pupils is of most value when they are given immediate and constructive feedback. For example, in a history lesson about the Tudors you might want to assess whether pupils have understood why Henry VIII wanted a divorce from his first wife, Catherine of Aragon. Questioning pupils about this may well reveal their level of understanding but will also provide an opportunity for you to put right any misunderstandings and reinforce points made in an earlier lesson. Having made a judgement about the level of understanding, you may wish to begin your next history lesson by revisiting these questions to ascertain how much has been retained and whether you need to go back over previously taught details.

Involving pupils in self-assessment

When pupils are themselves involved in assessing their own performance, they can often provide teachers and teaching assistants with insights into their own learning. Research has indicated that pupil involvement is likely to encourage pupils to become more focused upon the teacher's intended learning outcomes, helps them to become more aware of personal areas in which they have strengths and weaknesses and in some instances assists in the management of behaviour (Cooper 1993, Rose 1998). Assessment information is only of value when it is used to improve teaching or learning. Pupils need to know how they are progressing and appreciate being involved in discussions about their own learning. Even on an informal basis, as a teaching assistant you should find opportunities to engage pupils in discussions about how they feel they are getting on with their work. The use of assessment materials for such discussions can be helpful and re-assuring. For the pupil who is doing well, a discussion of an assessed piece of work may enable them to improve still further by developing those strengths which you are able to identify when talking to them. For the pupil who may be performing beneath their capability, a discussion about assessed work may enable you to provide those formative pointers which indicate how they could improve. Such discussions may also be important in protecting the self-esteem of pupils. If all of the information which pupils get about assessment is in the form of marks or comments in books how can they progress?

Case study

Clive is a year 3 pupil who has had some difficulties settling into his new school. The teacher has had concerns that his work in English is less competent than that of others in the school and is aware that he is beginning to dislike English lessons because he knows that he will find the work difficult. Yesterday Clive completed a short piece of work in his English book which was a review of a book he had been given for Christmas. The teacher had been impressed with Clive's obvious enthusiasm for this book but had commented to Shirley, the teaching assistant in her class, that she had assessed the work and the English was very poor.

Today Shirley went through this piece of work with Clive. She identified two points which she felt could help him to improve in his work. However, she began by talking to Clive about the book and built upon his enthusiasm for the story. She told him how impressed both she and the teacher were with his understanding of the text and that she would like to help him to improve the work so that he could share it with others in the class. She then indicated to him a couple of things which she felt they could do together to improve his work. Clive was very pleased to receive this support and attention and agreed that they should work on this aspect of improving his English work.

In this example, Shirley has been sensitive to Clive's feelings and has identified how the assessment information gathered can be used to assist her in helping Clive to improve his English. She demonstrates not only the importance of assessment, but also the necessity to think carefully about how pupils may best be supported in understanding their own learning needs in a sensitive and empathetic manner.

PRACTICAL TASK

After an assessment (such as a spelling test, or work returned to pupils after marking), talk to an individual pupil about the process. Ask them:

- why they believe teachers assess or mark their work;
- what they find helpful about this;
- how obtaining a good mark makes them feel;
- how getting a poor mark makes them feel.

After the discussion, consider how assessment in the pupil's class may be managed to ensure that it is supportive of pupil learning.

Record keeping

All teachers are required to maintain records which indicate the progress which pupils are making and their attainment as measured through formal assessment procedures. As a professional teaching assistant there is much that you can do to support this process. You should ensure that you are conversant with the school policies related to record keeping. If you know what teachers are expected to do, you will be more aware of the kind of information you can provide which will be valuable to them.

Many records will be cumulative and will indicate how pupils are progressing throughout the year. For example, teachers may keep records of weekly spelling tests, or end-of-term assessments in maths which indicate how pupils are doing and provides data which will identify any anomalies in terms of inconsistencies. You can make an important contribution to these records by ensuring that you record carefully all of the sessions which you do with groups or individual pupils. Teachers will set learning objectives for the sessions where you are working with pupils and will often expect you to assess pupils against these. As with all aspects of your work, communication with the teacher in order to be clear about these objectives is essential. It is important to devise a system for keeping records of the sessions which you manage which suits you. Bear in mind that you may be asked for information several days or even weeks after a session and therefore clarity will be an important factor in ensuring the effectiveness of the system. The following simple session-record, based upon a series of key questions, has been used by a group of teaching assistants working in a primary school.

Lesson focus:
What was the lesson objective(s)?
What did the pupils do?
What did they find easy?
What did they find hard?
Were the resources effective?
Was there any outstanding or poor pupil performance?

This simple set of questions enables the teaching assistant to focus upon the most important aspects of the lesson. They enable the teaching assistant to record events during the lesson which tells something about its success, the usefulness of resources and the performance of pupils. Such information can easily be retained and used for discussion with the class teacher as needed.

The topic of assessment is one of the most complex and contentious in education. It is important that you learn from the teachers with whom you are working. Each is likely to have their own preferred systems and records which suit their own approaches to teaching. At the same time, schools will have established procedures to which you will need to adhere. It is important that you keep yourself informed about these procedures and the inevitable changes to them which take place from time to time.

Summary

- Assessment is an ongoing process and should be an integral part of teaching.
- Accurate assessment information can enable you both to understand the progress and achievements of pupils and to plan for their future development.
- Comprehensive record keeping and communication with the class teacher should be an important function of your role as a teaching assistant.

References

Cooper, P (1993) Learning from pupils' perspectives. *British journal of special education* 20 (4) 129–33.

Department for Education and Skills (2001) *Special educational needs code of practice*. London: DfES.

Gipps, C (1993) The structure for assessment and recording, in O'Hear, P and White, J (eds) *Assessing the National Curriculum*. London: Paul Chapman.

Rose, R (1998) Including pupils: developing a partnership in learning, in Tilstone, C, Florian, L and Rose, R (eds) *Promoting inclusive practice*. London: Routledge.

Tilstone, C and Layton, L (2004) *Child development and teaching pupils with special educational needs*. London: Routledge Falmer.

9. Managing classroom behaviour

Introduction

All children (and adults) behave badly sometimes – this is part of human nature. However, some pupils cause particular anxiety to adults because of the persistency or intensity of the behaviours that they exhibit, and which present challenges to the teacher. Pupils behave badly for a number of reasons and there have been many texts written to try and analyse the causes of behaviour perceived as difficult or unacceptable (Fontana 1994, Cooper, Smith and Upton 1995). It is important that as a professional teaching assistant you try to understand the reasons for poor pupil behaviour. However, it is equally necessary to appreciate that this is a complex area and that there will be times when pupils behave in ways which appear inexplicable or, in some instances, are completely out of character. In this chapter while we will devote some time to trying to understand why pupils behave badly, we will be most concerned with a consideration of the ways in which your role can be supportive of teachers in the effective management of pupil behaviour.

The effective management of behaviour is greatly dependent upon the establishment of positive behaviour between adults and children (O'Brien 1998). That adults have high expectations of pupil behaviour and a positive attitude demonstrating that each individual pupil is valued and respected are critical starting points in achieving good behaviour management skills. Adults who expect poor behaviour and communicate this anxiety to pupils are more likely to experience difficulties and may even create situations of conflict and poor behaviour. It is important to recognise that behaviour can change, and that adults working in schools can have a significant impact upon improvements in this area. Simply accepting that a pupil has behaviour difficulties and that this cannot be changed is unacceptable. In some instances poor behaviour can have a detrimental effect upon the learning of the whole class. All teachers and teaching assistants therefore are under an obligation to make efforts both to manage and change behaviour effectively. McNamara and Moreton (1995) have clearly demonstrated that professional colleagues who accept the need to try different approaches to behaviour management and recognise that individual pupils or different situations may require a range of management techniques, are most likely to become effective managers of behaviour. These two authors also emphasis that, in many instances, adults will need to try a range of approaches before finding one which is most effective. If you find the behaviour of some pupils to be extremely challenging and sometimes feel that you don't know how to address situations which arise, remember that you are not alone. There are pupils who challenge the skills and understanding of the most experienced and well-organised teachers. It is important that you discuss the challenges which you face with your teacher colleagues and share their ideas in order to overcome problems. The teacher who says that they never have problems in managing behaviour is likely either to be unable to admit to the difficulties which they have encountered, or highly inexperienced. Most teachers will freely admit to having met pupils who challenge them through a range of behaviour which they find unacceptable or disturbing.

In this chapter we will consider how as a professional teaching assistant you may develop the essential skills required to support your teacher colleagues in the management of poor or disruptive behaviour. In particular, you will be asked to consider how your own behaviour, and the ways in which you work in the classroom, may have an impact upon the whole classroom ethos and the ways in which individuals and groups of pupils behave. This chapter will focus upon the standards highlighted in the box below.

HLTA STANDARDS

1.3 They demonstrate and promote the positive values, attitudes and behaviour they expect from the pupils with whom they work.

2.5 They know the key factors that can affect the way pupils learn.

2.9 They know a range of strategies to establish a purposeful learning environment and to promote good behaviour.

3.1.2 Working within a framework set by the teacher, they plan their role in lessons, including how they will provide feedback to pupils and colleagues on pupils' learning and behaviour.

3.3.2 They communicate effectively and sensitively with pupils to support their learning.

3.3.4 They use behaviour management strategies, in line with the school's policy and procedures, which contribute to a purposeful learning environment.

CHAPTER OBJECTIVES

By the end of this chapter you should:

- have an understanding of some of the causes of challenging pupil behaviour;
- have identified how your own role can be developed to provide effective support to the classroom teacher in managing difficult behaviour;
- have considered how your own attitudes and behaviours can impact upon the behaviour of pupils;
- have considered a range of techniques and approaches which may assist in the management of pupil behaviour.

98

Creating an environment which supports positive behaviour

All schools are required to have a behaviour policy which should establish the expectations of teachers and other staff and provide clear guidance on behaviour management. It is important that all staff, including teaching assistants, are fully conversant with this policy. If you are unfamiliar with the school's behaviour policy, you should ask for a copy and discuss it with the teachers with whom you work. The school policy should describe the means through which positive behaviour is promoted throughout the school. This is not simply a matter of how staff will deal with unacceptable behaviour, but should be focused upon the conditions created in school to encourage pupils to behave well. Effective schools have rules with which all staff and pupils are familiar. In many schools these are posted clearly around the building as a reminder to the whole school community. However, rules alone are insufficient in creating an ethos conducive to good behaviour. Every adult in the school must work towards establishing a level of consistency with regards to expectation of pupils and the ways in which they treat the individuals in their charge. The actions of adults will have a significant influence upon the ways in which pupils both view the school and behave. As a professional teaching assistant, you can do much through your own attitude and behaviour to encourage good behaviour in pupils. Several writers (Gray and Richer 1988, Derrington and Groom 2004) have identified the following professional skills as crucial for the promotion of high pupil self-esteem and good behaviour.

Trusting pupils and establishing respect

Pupils will respond most positively if they feel that they are valued by the adults who are working with them. You can achieve this by showing interest in what they do both within school and in their life outside. It is important that pupils regard you as being approachable and willing to listen to what they have to say. This does not necessarily mean that you will always accept their opinions but that you are always prepared to adopt their point of view. From very early in their lives, children develop a keen sense of what is fair. If they perceive you to be someone who deals with them fairly, they are likely to respect you and appreciate your role within the school.

Behaving consistently towards pupils

Most of us feel more comfortable when we know that we can expect a consistent reaction from the people around us. Since we are adults and have individual opinions and ideas about how pupils should behave, consistency across the school is very difficult to achieve. However, as individuals we can all play an important role in enabling pupils to understand our personal expectations and attitudes. Pupils are more likely to stay within the parameters of what you see as acceptable behaviour if you are giving them consistent signals about your expectations. If a pupil acts in a particular way on one occasion and you tell them that this is unacceptable but on another day you ignore or accept this same behaviour, then they cannot be expected to understand the rules to which you are working. It is vital that you maintain an approach which clearly informs pupils about what is expected of them and that you apply this expectation with consistency. It is equally important that pupils know why certain behaviour is unacceptable. Taking the time to talk about rules and the consequences of unacceptable behaviour is an important part of the process of encouraging pupil self-discipline.

Recognising individuality and the differing experiences of pupils

Pupils do not all have the same experience of expectations regarding their behaviour. We know that the home situation plays a major part in influencing the ways in which pupils behave, and that different parents have a range of expectations of their children. It takes time for pupils to learn and understand rules and to know what is expected of them. This is, of course, where achieving consistency is so important. As a professional teaching assistant you will, from time to time, hear criticisms of the ways in which parents manage their children's behaviour. Some of this criticism will be valid but will be of little value in assisting with behaviour management. Recognising the individuality of pupils and the different experiences which they have had, is critical in enabling them to come to understand the expectations regarding behaviour in the school situation. This understanding will best be achieved by staff who are non-judgemental but take a positive stance in supporting pupils so that they can come to see the importance and value of the school's rules and adult expectations. You must learn to listen to pupils and to provide them with opportunities to discuss the ways in which they interpret the expectations of the school in order to achieve high levels of acceptable behaviour.

Working consistently within existing school policies and rules

School managers establish policies and rules for the efficient running of the school. In becoming conversant with and applying these rules, you will be supporting the development of an ethos which encourages positive pupil behaviour. Many schools have introduced systems of rewards and sanctions to assist in the management of behaviour. These only work well when they are consistently applied. This demands that staff have the same interpretation of the rewards and sanctions system in order to apply this in a way which pupils regard as fair. If you work regularly with one particular teacher, it is often easier to gain a consistency of approach. This is less easily achieved when working with a range of adults who have differing interpretations of school rules and policies. Always be prepared to discuss interpretation with teachers but, more importantly, having agreed upon the way in which policies and rules should be applied, make sure that you do so as consistently as possible.

Emphasising pupil achievement

Pupils who are successful in school and in their academic achievements are less likely to behave badly. When pupils gain success they feel comfortable and good about themselves. All pupils, regardless of need or ability, need to feel that they are making progress. Sometimes this may be difficult for them to perceive. Pupils who may, for example, have special educational needs, may become very frustrated with their own lack of progress and may begin to feel resentment of teachers or the school as a whole. When pupils are not succeeding, they may need to find someone to blame or may begin to rebel against the system in which they feel that they are failing. As a professional teaching assistant you can do much to help pupils overcome this situation. You must identify what pupils are doing well and point this out to them as often as possible. Provide praise for pupil achievement, even when this may be small when compared to that of their peers. However, be careful to only praise real progress or achievement, as pupils will quickly learn not to trust you if they think that you lack sincerity. Learning and behaviour are inextricably linked. Pupils who behave badly are less likely to learn effectively and may in fact impinge upon the learning of others. Those who recognise their own successes are more likely to behave well and to continue to make progress.

PRACTICAL TASK

Examine the school's behaviour policy and look in particular at what this says about rewards and sanctions. Think carefully about how you interpret this policy and what you do to support its implementation.

Involve a small group of pupils in a discussion about this policy. Do they interpret the school rules and the system of rewards and sanctions in the same way as you do?

What do you feel we can learn from such discussions with pupils, and how might the information gained be used to support the maintenance of good behaviour in school?

Who behaves badly and why?

At the beginning of this chapter we stated that all children behave badly sometimes. However, there are some pupils whose behaviour seems always to present a challenge to teachers. It is important that we consider why pupils behave badly and recognise those causal factors which are either directly within our ability to control or result from conditions which are more complex.

Some pupils will exhibit challenging behaviours related to a special educational need. For example, there are some pupils within the autistic spectrum who, as a result of their difficulties with communication and an inability to make normal social contact with their peers or adults, present challenging behaviours which can be directly attributed to their difficulties. It is, however, important not to form stereotypical views of pupils simply because they have been given a label. Not all pupils with autistic spectrum disorders will present a major behavioural problem. Your expectations of pupils are important and must be based upon your experience of the individual rather than upon pre-conceived opinions of how pupils described by labels such as autism may behave. While some pupils will certainly have considerable difficulties in managing their own behaviour, this does not diminish the importance of the adults working with them having consistent strategies for their management.

Some pupils, whose behaviour may be extreme, may have a statement of special educational needs (*see* Chapters 7 and 8), which identifies the resources and approaches required to assist staff in their management and education. Such pupils may be described as having social, emotional and behavioural difficulties (SEBD), or may have a more specific diagnosis such as Attention Deficit Hyperactivity Disorder (ADHD). It is essential that you familiarise yourself with the contents of the statements given to such pupils and that you are fully aware of the management expectations put in place for them. Where behaviour difficulties are extreme, consistency is a critical factor in promoting effective management. You may find that individual behaviour programmes or specific approaches to the management of rewards and sanctions are in place for an individual pupil. You must adhere to these and be seen to be supportive of teachers in their implementation. It is equally important to remember that you may bring a different perspective to understanding such pupils. You may work much more intensively than the class teacher with a pupil with challenging behaviours and may therefore observe behaviours and reactions which the teacher has little opportunity to recognise. It is vital that you record such observations and share them with the teacher as they may be of considerable benefit in enabling the pupil to learn successfully.

It is of particular importance that you take note of any behaviour which is out of character or unusual in specific individual pupils. Sometimes a pupil's behaviour changes as a consequence of events or occurrences in their lives. If a pupil who normally behaves well suddenly begins to behave badly, then there is likely to be a reason for this. We often hear adults refer to a pupil behaving badly as 'attention seeking'. When a normally well-behaved pupil behaves badly this may indeed be a case of seeking additional attention and should *not* be ignored. Pupils who are experiencing some form of trauma such as family breakdown or bereavement are likely to need extra attention from adults and in some instances they may obtain this through behaviour which is inconsistent with their usual character. If you observe a situation in which a pupil is behaving in a way which is unusual for them, you should discuss this with a teacher in order to ensure that the pupil receives the support which they need. In situations such as these, pupils need to feel well supported and to know that you care about their feelings and emotions. The management of behaviour which is related to changed circumstances or personal trauma is highly dependent upon the ability of an adult to empathise, to listen carefully and to demonstrate an understanding of the personal circumstances of the individual concerned.

The demands of the school and the ways in which pupils interpret these should never be underestimated. There may be times when pupils experience difficulties with the work put before them and feel that they cannot learn or that they are not coping with the situation. Where pupils feel that they are failing they are more likely to behave badly. Most learners feel more confident in some subjects and some learning situations than in others. It is not unusual for a pupil to behave consistently well in some lessons while they appear always to misbehave in others. Often this will be associated with their level of confidence with the learning materials. In some cases it may be about their relationship with the teacher. Teaching assistants can often do much to boost the confidence of pupils and to avoid situations of conflict or unacceptable behaviour.

Case study

Jenny has recently returned to school following three weeks absence through illness. She is clearly pleased to be back in school with her friends and has been generally well behaved. However, during the past three maths lessons, when working in a group with other pupils she has been uncooperative and at times has disrupted the work of the group. Yesterday, her behaviour became so unacceptable that the teacher removed her from the group and insisted that she sit alone to do her work. At the end of the lesson she had completed only a small part of the work and incurred the displeasure of the teacher who told her that she was dissatisfied with her performance. During break, Wendy, the teaching assistant who works in Jenny's class, sat with her and talked about how she felt her return to school was going. Jenny discussed all of the good things, such as being back with her friends and not being bored at home. After a little encouragement from Wendy, Jenny began to talk about how she felt about missing quite a lot of work, particularly in maths.

Wendy discussed Jenny's anxieties with the teacher and together they planned a series of activities for Wendy to do with Jenny during morning registration to help her to catch up with the maths which she had missed. Wendy discussed this plan with Jenny and together over the next two weeks they worked together each morning to help Jenny catch up with what she had missed.

In the case study above, a number of factors were important. First, Wendy, the teaching assistant, recognised that Jenny's behaviour was out of character and that she was behaving badly in a particular situation, in this case maths lessons. Following this, Wendy took the time to engage Jenny in discussion, to listen to what she had to say about her return to school and to empathise over her difficulties. Finally, along with the teacher, Wendy took positive action to assist Jenny in addressing her difficulties, thus showing that her earlier expressed concern was being followed up in a way which Jenny could see as supportive.

Clearly, not all behaviour difficulties will be so easily diagnosed or addressed. It is, however, essential that as a professional teaching assistant you play a role in assisting teachers in the management of behaviour. There will be times when you notice things that teachers miss. This is not, however, a criticism of teachers who have to address a wide range of demands and are usually working under considerable pressure. Your communication with the teacher may be a critical factor in enabling behaviour difficulties to be managed.

Planning to be an effective manager of behaviour

The effective management of behaviour is something which all teachers find challenging but involves skills and processes which we can all learn. We have already discussed some of the principles of behaviour management, such as consistency and communication, which are crucial components in enabling schools to develop as effective learning environments. At the day-to-day level there are many procedures which you can put in place which will assist you in becoming an effective manager of behaviour.

When planning to work with pupils it helps to try and identify those parts of a lesson or activity which are potentially problematic. By being well prepared you may be able to avoid difficulties and create a teaching situation which is more conducive to learning. Being well prepared and confident is a significant factor in preventing classroom misbehaviour. A series of key questions may assist with this process.

Do any of the pupils have specific behavioural difficulties and targets set to address them?

Some pupils with behavioural difficulties will have a behaviour management programme which identifies specific targets. Be aware of these and try to identify opportunities to address them in your sessions. It often helps to discuss these with the pupil at the beginning of the session to remind them of your expectations. Don't forget to give feedback to the pupil about how well they did in relation to the targets during the session.

Are there pupils in this group who work well together, and conversely, others who do not?

Think about how and where you will seat pupils before the session starts. If you have pupils who don't work well together try to keep them apart or, if they must work together, remind them of your expectations before you begin work. Give praise when pupils work well together.

Do I have all of the resources, that I require for this session?

If you have to leave a group to collect materials, this is a time for potential disruption. Be well organised and think through each stage of the session in advance to ensure that everything you need is to hand.

How will I arrange the learning situation?

When planning a session think about how long pupils will be able to concentrate on specific aspects of the tasks set. To maintain interest, it often helps to vary the tasks and the materials used. If you know that you are working with pupils who have a limited attention span, be prepared to give them a range of short activities addressing the same learning outcomes. Give similar consideration to the positioning of pupils. Do they have easy access to the materials they will need? Can they see quite clearly any resources which you are demonstrating or trying to show them? Are they seated comfortably so that they have no need to keep moving? These may seem like minor points but they can make a considerable difference.

What will I communicate to all pupils and to individuals about my expectations?

Pupils need to be sure about what you want them to do. This may not be the same for all pupils so you should spend time making your expectations clear. Do not expect all of the pupils to remember what you have asked of them. Regular reminders will help all pupils to stay on task. It is often helpful to stop the session to help pupils refocus. Do this by using the pupils' own work, showing everyone what they have done and praising them for their efforts. Reiterate your expectations and allow pupils to proceed feeling good about what they are doing.

Do I have enough materials for the whole session?

If you have a 40-minute session with a group of pupils and they complete their work after 20 minutes, the next 20 minutes is potentially a difficult time for them and for you. Try to have a series of extension activities and supplementary materials to hand. You may not use them during the session but they can be useful if pupils finish work early and need to be kept purposefully occupied.

It is important to remember that effective behaviour management has to be learned. All good teachers will admit to having experienced difficulties with behaviour management at some point in their careers. You should not expect the effective management of behaviour to be something which you acquire without working hard to develop the necessary skills. In this chapter we have discussed a series of principles which are intended to encourage you to think about yourself as a manager of behaviour. By considering your own actions and discussing these with professional colleagues and with pupils, you can develop the necessary skills of behaviour management which are an essential component of every well-managed classroom.

PRACTICAL TASK

Examine a plan for a group activity which you will be supervising in the near future. For each pupil in that group, ask the following questions:

- Are there particular parts of this session which this pupil will find difficult?
- Does the pupil have specific behaviour targets? Do I know what these are? How will I ensure that these are addressed?
- Will this pupil require materials which are additional to or different from those provided for their peers?
- Who will this pupil work well with?
- Is there anybody who this pupil will not work well with?
- What do I expect the pupil to learn?
- How will I communicate these expectations to the pupil?
- How will I let him know about the progress which he is making?

When you have answered these questions for each pupil, plan the session in a way which takes full consideration of your answers. Check and discuss your planning with the class teacher.

Summary

Effective behaviour management is dependent upon:

- good communication between teaching assistants and teachers;
- an ability to listen to the views of pupils;
- high expectations of all pupils with respect to both learning and behaviour;
- being well organised for all teaching situations;
- providing work which is at a level appropriate to pupil needs;
- having consistent expectations and reactions to behaviours;
- being seen to be fair;
- recognising individuality;
- knowing and consistently applying school policies.

References

Cooper, P, Smith, C and Upton, G (1995) *Emotional and behavioural difficulties – theory to practice*. London: Routledge.

Derrington, C and Groom, B (2004) *A team approach to behaviour management*. London: Paul Chapman.

Fontana, D (1994) *Managing classroom behaviour*. Leicester: British Psychological Society.

Gray, J and Richer, J (1998) *Classroom responses to disruptive behaviour*. London: Macmillan.

McNamara, S and Moreton, G (1995) *Changing behaviour*. London: David Fulton.

O'Brien, T (1998) *Promoting positive behaviour*. London: David Fulton.

www.behaviour4learning.ac.uk

10. Learning beyond the classroom

Introduction

While the classroom provides the focus of much learning in the lives of children, it is important to remember that there are many learning opportunities available in other situations. Pupils attend school for only a limited period of time each week and it would be naïve to assume that they are not continuing to learn when they are away from the classroom. Similarly, while the image which many of us have of formal education is of pupils seated in classrooms engaging in activities managed by adults, we need to be aware of the many additional opportunities which exist to extend pupils' learning through visits and other activities which are managed by the school but in a different learning environment. Most schools will organise visits and, in some instances, residential learning experiences for pupils. When well managed these can be a rewarding and beneficial experience for all involved. However, they do need to be carefully planned and implemented in order to ensure that all pupils gain maximum learning benefits from the experience.

While many of the same principles for effective teaching which are applied in the classroom hold good for the management of learning in other situations, there are important considerations which need to be given to promoting a safe and rewarding experience out of school. Pupils who have learned the rules and social mores of learning in a classroom may at times have difficulty transferring these to other learning situations. Where this is the case, there is a need to ensure that the adults working with them provide clear guidance and management. Similarly, pupils who have learned about the limited risks which exist within a classroom environment may not be so well attuned to those which exist out of school. The need for vigilance in attending to health and safety issues cannot be over emphasised when planning and conducting learning outside of the classroom.

In this chapter we will consider the development of good practice in recognising learning opportunities beyond the classroom. This will include a consideration of the ways in which we can use the individual experiences which different pupils have and bring with them to school, as well as examining the development of principles which will enable you to support pupil learning on school visits. In particular the chapter will focus upon the standards highlighted in the box below.

HLTA STANDARDS

2.9   They know a range of strategies to establish a purposeful learning environment and to promote good behaviour.

3.1.1 They contribute effectively to teachers' planning and preparation of lessons.

3.1.4 They are able to contribute to the planning of opportunities for pupils to learn in out-of-school contexts, in accordance with school policies and procedures.

3.3.1 Using clearly structured teaching and learning activities, they interest and motivate pupils, and advance their learning.

3.3.4 They use behaviour management strategies, in line with the school's policy and procedures, which contribute to a purposeful learning environment.

3.3.8 They organise and manage safely the learning activities, the physical teaching space and resources for which they are given responsibility.

CHAPTER OBJECTIVES

By the end of this chapter you should:

● appreciate the importance of valuing the wide range of learning which pupils experience outside of the classroom;

● have considered how your own role in supporting colleagues on school visits may be most effectively developed;

● understand the principles which determine effective planning and implementation of out-of-school activities.

Recognising the experiences of the pupil

What do the pupils with whom you work do when they are not at school? In many ways it is good to be able to stop thinking about these pupils once they have left your care, but getting to know something about what they do outside of school hours may provide useful opportunities in the classroom. Most of the pupils with whom you work will have interests, hobbies and experiences which provide them with unique learning. For example, you are likely to work with pupils who attend cubs or brownies, play for local football teams, attend a church or mosque, have swimming or music lessons, collect various items or regularly watch specific television programmes. Each of these experiences will provide a range of learning opportunities and may enable pupils to gain skills, knowledge and understanding in a more effective way than would be possible in the classroom. However, this learning can often be related to the classroom situation and may in some instances be turned to your advantage when working with pupils.

At the most basic level, it is important that pupils feel that you are interested in them, value their lives outside of school and respect their interests and experiences. A pupil who has been to watch her favourite football team at the weekend may well arrive in school wanting to tell you all about the trip and her experiences. By making time to listen to this pupil, even if you personally have no interest in football, you are showing that you are interested in her as an individual and that you value her ideas and experiences. Many schools provide opportunities at registration, or through the use of circle time, to enable pupils to share their news and interests with others. This is important to the pupils and should also be regarded as a useful opportunity for staff to get to know the pupils better and to identify ways in which they may build upon the interests of their class. In some instances you may be able to use a pupil's personal experiences to advantage in the classrooms. The following case study shows how one teaching assistant made effective use of the experiences of an individual pupil.

Case study

During registration on a Monday morning, Kevin tells the class about a visit he made on Saturday with his parents to the National Space Centre near Leicester. He is clearly excited about what he saw at the centre and about some of the interactive experiences which he enjoyed during the visit. In particular, he was impressed by the rocket tower which housed two real rockets. While at the centre he had drawn a picture of these rockets and, encouraged by the teacher, he has promised to bring these, along with a souvenir booklet, into school to show everybody the next day. None of the other class members have been to the National Space Centre but they are all interested in what Kevin has to say and by his enthusiasm.

On Tuesday Kevin brings to school his drawings, a souvenir brochure and a model of one of the rockets which he had purchased at the centre shop. Samantha, the teaching assistant in Kevin's class, makes a small area for displaying these materials on a worktop in the classroom, and Kevin agrees that at various times during the day pupils can take these from the display to look at them.

Later in the week, Samantha is working with a group of pupils in a religious education lesson in which they are discussing special books. They have looked at books associated with specific religions, in particular the Bible, the Qur'an and the Torah. Samantha asks the pupils about how they might help others to know about the importance of these books and what they contain. One pupil suggests that they could produce a guide to the books, like the one which Kevin brought in from the Space Centre. Samantha agrees that this is a good idea and fetches the guidebook from the Space Centre to discuss with the pupils. They look at this and consider how information is presented (in written and pictorial form), what makes it interesting and how a similar approach could be used to introduce one of the special books. After some discussion the pupils agree to produce a guide to the Bible which will tell people who are unfamiliar with the book something about its contents and why it is important.

Using the National Space Centre souvenir guide as a stimulus, the pupils produce their own guidebook. At the end of the day they share this with other members of the class and discuss how they used the guidebook brought in by Kevin to develop their own ideas.

In the case study which you have just read an initial link between Kevin's visit to the National Space Centre and the religious education lesson was, at best, tenuous. However, Samantha has used her initiative and, in recognising the enthusiasm that the class had shown towards the materials provided by Kevin, she maintained their interest in this activity. In so doing, she has not only developed an interesting approach to meeting the lesson objectives, but has also enabled pupils to use their own initiative, has emphasised the value of the learning opportunities available outside of school and demonstrated to Kevin the value of his personal learning experience.

Pupils need to be encouraged to recognise that learning is not simply something that happens in schools. Kelly (1995) has demonstrated that a more holistic view of education recognises the value of all experiences as being inter-related as an educational process. He emphasises that what pupils know and learn cannot be divorced from their personality and interests and, that it is important to incorporate those things which we want pupils to learn as closely as possible into those aspects of their lives which they perceive as being most important. This can only be achieved when we truly know our pupils and appreciate their individual interests and motivations.

Opportunities to make use of pupil interests exist in every classroom and good teachers recognise and develop these wherever possible. The value of this approach cannot be underestimated. Not only does it recognise and appreciate the experiences which pupils may have gained outside of school, but it also provides the teacher or teaching assistant with an effective means of maintaining pupil enthusiasm and developing more innovative teaching methods.

PRACTICAL TASK

How much do you know about the interests and enthusiasms of the pupils with whom you regularly work? Identify a group of pupils who you know and complete the chart for each of them? (Extend the length of the chart as necessary.)

PUPIL	OUT OF SCHOOL INTEREST

Now give the pupils a blank copy of this chart and ask them to complete it for their classmates. Do they know much about each other?

When you have collected all of this information answer the following questions.

● Are the interests of pupils and the learning opportunities which these present ever discussed in class?

● Can I see any opportunities to develop my own teaching in respect of some of these pupil interests?

Recognising that much of what pupils learn takes place outside of school in informal situations is important. Equally critical is the recognition that learning which takes place in school needs to relate to the outside world. Most of us respond best to teaching when we can see its relevance to our own lives. As adults we often make choices about what we want to learn in ways which are not widely available to the pupils in our classrooms. As a professional teaching assistant you have many opportunities to demonstrate to pupils how the things which they are learning in school may serve them well in other situations. This may include providing examples of how, for example, the mathematics which pupils have learned could be used in relation to an interest or hobby which they may have. It will not always be possible to provide such concrete examples but, by demonstrating how the learning which pupils achieve in the classroom may be related to their everyday lives, you are more likely to foster a greater enthusiasm for school-based learning.

Supporting school visits

Trips. Let's go!

We all love trips and we can learn so much from going out and seeing things.

Numeracy hour and literacy hour can be so boring. LET US OUT!

The teachers and the children would love more organised outings, but I bet the Department of Education says no. In other countries the less formal approach is very successful, so why not give it a go?

Kimberley (11 years old)
(Burke and Grosvenor 2003)

As suggested by the pupil quoted above, school visits can be an enjoyable and rewarding experience for pupils and staff alike. They can act as a stimulus for further work at school, can be used to verify and strengthen understanding based upon previously taught lessons and they provide an opportunity for pupils to gain new experiences and understanding of the world. Many of the subjects which are taught in school demand that pupils gain an understanding of ideas which may appear abstract or obscure but which may be illuminated through the use of school visits. For example, in religious education an appreciation of the rituals and beliefs expressed in the Sikh religion may be greatly enhanced by a visit to a gudwara; an understanding of the ways in which artists work may be supported through a visit to a studio or gallery; or insights into how the Ancient Egyptians lived may be gained by time spent at a museum. Visits can provide pupils with a chance to handle artefacts, engage in interactive approaches to learning and meet with experts in a way which it is often difficult to provide in school.

Planning and organisation

Some schools have now appointed educational visits co-ordinators who take responsibility for overseeing the effective organisation of all school visits. This will include the essential management of health and safety considerations. Most schools have comprehensive school visits policies and many will have carefully prepared checklists for use by staff. You should ensure that you are familiar with these documents. In recent years there has been an increased concern about the risks to both staff and pupils which can be faced when undertaking a school visit. These concerns have been well publicised and follow a number of tragic incidents involving pupils and staff. However, you should remember that so long as the appropriate guidelines are followed, the vast majority of school visits will be uneventful and successful. This does not mean that staff can afford to be complacent when planning a school visit. There are a number of helpful guidance documents which schools typically use in order to ensure that their planning takes account of health and safety issues. In 1998 the (now) Department for Education and Skills issued *Health and Safety of Pupils on Educational Visits: A Good Practice Guide,* a document with which you should become familiar. Several of the teaching unions have produced similar guidance to which teachers will adhere. It is advisable that you discuss with teachers their interpretation and compliance with these important health and safety documents.

When planning an educational visit there are a number of procedures that need to be followed. These will generally be the responsibility of the teacher in charge of the visit, or in some cases will be undertaken by the educational visits co-ordinator. The following checklist was completed by staff who were planning a visit to a local museum to support their history about the Romans in Britain.

ST MARKS'S ST SCHOOL VISIT PLANNING SHEET

To be completed prior to all school visits and approved by the head teacher.

Visit to: City Museum Date: October 28th

Purpose: To examine Roman artefacts

Class: 6L   Number of pupils: 29   Teacher in charge: Anne Lambert

1. PUPILS	ACTION	COMPLETED (PLEASE DATE)
Letter to parents	Send letter to parents/carers of all pupils involved in visit along with consent forms	Oct 7th
Consent forms received	Consent forms required for *all* pupils to be taken on visit	Last one received Oct 16th
Specific pupil needs	Mary will need to take inhaler Sunil requires lunchtime medication	Checked on the day Oct 28th
2. STAFFING		
Selection of staff and other adults	Two teaching assistants, Jane Riley and Philip Bates, will attend. Three parent volunteers – Mrs Key, Mrs Watts and Mrs Kumble	Confirmed Oct 8th
Staff briefed	Lunchtime meeting arranged with all adults going on visit.	Oct 16th
3. THE VENUE		
Preliminary visit made by staff	Anne Lambert and Jane Riley visited museum after school one evening	Sept 20th
Education materials collected from venue	Education packs collected during preliminary visit	Sept 20th
Contact with education officer (where appropriate)	Discussion with education officer during preliminary visit. She is available for the day of the visit	Sept 20th
4. TRANSPORT		
Getting to and from venue	Coach booked with Sherwin coaches and confirmed	Sept 24th
Departure/return arrangements	Leave school 9.15 am. Return 3.00 pm. (within school day)	
5. LUNCHTIME ARRANGEMENTS	All pupils asked to bring packed lunches. Reminder letter sent	Oct 25th
6. HEALTH & SAFETY		
Completion of risk assessment form	Completed with Mr Radbourne (Health and Safety Officer)	Oct 16th

The form above is just one example of the type of planning procedure typically used in schools today. Your school may well have a different format but the content is not likely to differ greatly from that shown here. You should ask to see a copy of your school's planning form and make sure that you are familiar with the expected procedures; you should also find out who oversees health and safety issues in your school.

There are some particular points from this planning procedure which need to be emphasised. You will note the importance attached to parental consent. Schools need to obtain the consent of parents or carers before taking pupils out of school. This generally means written consent. Schools are responsible for ensuring that parents are conversant with the purpose of the school visit. They will be greatly reassured if the school provides as much detail as possible, particularly about levels of staffing and safety issues. For some parents or carers it may be necessary to provide information in their home language. It may often be useful to support a letter with a telephone call if you are uncertain about whether parents will understand the information sent out.

On the form presented above there is a section which refers to specific pupil needs. This should be given early consideration as it may involve staff in planning how to manage a situation prior to the visit. In this case it acts as a reminder that Mary will need to take her inhaler with her and that someone will need to be responsible for ensuring that Sunil takes his lunchtime medication. In some instances there may be a need for more detailed planning. For example, if you have a pupil who is a wheelchair user, you will need to consider access and the availability of disabled toileting facilities. This is one reason why a preliminary visit to the venue may be of particular importance. While it may not always be possible to make such a visit, the gathering of as much information as possible before the visit will enable you to anticipate where there may be difficulties and will also provide you with information about what you want the pupils to see when they arrive.

As a professional teaching assistant you may be able to take responsibility for some parts of this planning and organisation. However, the teacher in charge has the main responsibility for ensuring that the visit is properly planned and that all necessary consent and precautions have been taken.

During the visit

As mentioned earlier, pupils who have become familiar with the expectations and rules of a school sometimes have difficulties with transferring these to out-of-school situations. Teachers often report that, while they value school visits, they find them quite stressful and exhausting. This is partly because they too are working in a less familiar environment and feel that the potential for things going wrong is increased. There is no reason why your school visit should not be completely successful but there is a need for increased vigilance on the part of all who are involved.

Some pupils will see the fact that they are out of school as meaning that the standards of behaviour expected in the classroom do not apply. Briefing pupils on your expectations before the visit is important. The pupils and the staff and volunteers with them are representing the school in a public forum and clearly you do not want them to let the school down. Reminding pupils about expectations in respect of behaviour and praising them for good conduct during the visit is important. Think carefully about how you allocate pupils to groups, trying to anticipate those who may not work well together and keeping them apart. Careful planning for how the time will be used during the visit can eliminate a number of problems. Pupils should arrive at the venue with a clear idea of the purpose of the visit and with tasks to be completed during this time. This does not mean giving them a clipboard with a tick list, which they then carry around with them. Where this approach is adopted it often results in pupils simply going quickly around the venue ticking boxes and paying little attention to detail.

The visit is an important teaching opportunity and as such needs to be planned in the same way as any lesson. The following plan was put together by the teacher who organised the museum visit outlined above.

VISIT SCHEDULE

9.00	Talk to all pupils about expectations during the day. Re-emphasise the information to be gathered and stress the importance of appropriate behaviour.
9.15	Check all pupils and adults onto coach.
9.45	Arrive museum. Meet education officer. Take all pupils into education room. Introduce them to education officer. Allocate groups to adults.
10.00	Talk by education officer
10.30	Drinks
10.45	Split pupils into three groups. Groups rotate between visiting museum and working with education officer in half-hour blocks.
12.30	Lunch
1.15	Watch video about Roman city, followed by final walk around museum.
2.00	Depart on coach for school.

During the visit, as a professional teaching assistant, you should be looking for ideas and teaching points which can be followed up back in school. Good communication with the class teacher is essential. On return to school you will have information which you have gained from the visit which needs to be shared with the teacher. While at the venue you will need to encourage pupils' learning by asking a series of pertinent questions which enable them to maintain a focus upon the intended learning outcomes. This means that you must be familiar with these outcomes prior to the visit. Do not assume that pupils see everything that you observe. By asking them questions you can focus their attention and enable them to get the most out of the experience.

PRACTICAL TASK

The next time there is a visit arranged for pupils from your school, take the opportunity to follow the procedures through. Focus upon the following questions.

- Are there established forms used by the staff?
- What was the purpose of the visit?
- What are the health and safety issues associated with this visit?
- How is the visit staffed?
- Who makes the arrangements?
- How was consent obtained?
- Was use made of an education officer or other expert?
- How was the visit followed up in school?

If possible discuss these questions with the member of staff who was in charge of the visit.

Summary

- There are many opportunities for learning which take place out of school.
- Pupils' out-of-school learning needs to be acknowledged, appreciated and celebrated.
- Good out-of-school learning experiences are based upon careful preparation and planning.
- Pupils will not always respond to a learning environment away from school as they do to the classroom situation. This requires that all out-of-school experiences are well staffed and that staff set clear guidelines of expectations for pupils.

References

Burke, C and Grosvenor, I (2003) *The school I'd like*. London: Routledge.

Department for Education and Skills (1998) *Health and safety of pupils on educational visits: a good practice guide*. London: DfES.

Kelly, GA (1995) *A theory of personality: the psychology of personal constructs*. New York: Norton Library.

Appendix: Case studies of HLTA candidates' assessments

The aim of these case studies is to help you to prepare for assessment of HLTA. Whichever route you choose, you will have to complete the same tasks.

At the end of Chapter 1 you undertook a self-review against the standards. This should be used now to help you identify situations which you could use for Tasks 1–4. Tasks 1–3 require you to outline and evaluate your experiences of working within everyday school classroom routines: first with an individual pupil, secondly with a small group and thirdly with a whole class.

Task 4 gives you an opportunity to look at five situations or events that provide evidence for standards not already covered. It is essential that you plan your Tasks 1–3 together and by doing this you will have covered most standards. You can then plan your Task 4 situations so that you can meet any remaining standards

Most candidates for HLTA status produce a number of drafts prior to submitting their final draft for assessment purposes. This level of preparation is essential as the assessor will use this draft as a way of identifying the standards that you clearly appear to meet and those standards that should be the focus of further investigation in the school visit. The style of writing used is for you to decide; some candidates use lists of asterisked or numbered points while others use continuous prose. It is essential that you focus on the standards in your drafts without simply repeating the same words of these standards. Let us now look at the first case study and in this case look at Task 1, working with an individual pupil.

Case study 1

Paul works in an 11–18 school in the SEN department. He undertook the assessment only course having done a range of courses for teaching assistants over the past five years.

Annex F1: Response sheet for task 1: Working with an individual pupil

1. Your details

Name	
Your area(s) of expertise for this task	
School	
Name of teacher for this task	

Where relevant in the following sections, the right-hand column is provided for you to record which Standards have been met.

2. Sources of evidence for this task

Document reference no.	Brief Description	Std		
T1-A	Lesson outcome – modifying approach	3.2.2		
T1-B	Statement – multi-sensory approach	2.7		
T1-C	Worksheet – cut and stuck for left-hand use	3.1.3		
T1-D	Lesson spelling test – cross-curricular	3.1.4		
T1-E	Worksheet – praise and merit stamp	3.3.4		
T1-F	Worksheet – self-correction	3.2.3		
T1-G	Notes to a colleague	3.3.6		
T1-H	Assessment included in Annual Review	1.5		
T1-I	Witness statement – managing resources	3.3.8		
T1-J	Annual spelling test – marked and compared with National spelling age.	2.2		

3. Context
A brief, but anonymous, profile of the pupil with whom you have been working:

The student I have been working with during this activity is a male aged 11 in Year 7. He has a Statement of Educational Need relating to difficulties caused by dyslexia. He is from a stable family background and is the 3rd of 3 children.

Working with the long-term aim to improve his reading and spelling skills to enable him to access the curriculum independently, he followed a commercial scheme called 'Beating Dyslexia'. The course of lessons used printed worksheets, a tape with step-by-step instructions, a foam alphabet and a blank tape to record, listen and write. The short-term targets during the weeks covered in this activity were to set out the alphabet without any errors, recognise letters and correctly spell selected words.

4.	Std
I contributed to the planning of this activity in the following ways:	
• I selected worksheets that would be completed during each session, the number of sheets I selected was adjusted by the number of sheets he had completed in the previous lesson and any difficulties he had experienced. The difficulties would be worked on at the expense of finishing other sheets (T1–A). Any errors he made were corrected at the time so the correction could be reinforced and he was left with a feeling of success.	3.3.5 3.1.3 3.2.2 3.3.3
• I organised photocopies from the 'Beating Dyslexia' master copies, with photocopying permission, adapting the handwriting sheets to allow for his left-hand writing position by cutting the sheet, reversing the columns and photocopying again (T1–C). I did this because he had to keep lifting his arm to copy and it interrupted the fluency of his handwriting.	3.1.3 3.2.2
• I made sure that there was a classroom available to ensure a quiet area with an electricity socket and whiteboard (T1–I). A quiet area was necessary as he was using the brightly coloured foam letters that were similar to a primary school type resource and this caused him embarrassment in front of his peers. I selected the foam letters for his use as they are a good kinaesthetic resource. His statement advised using different multi-sensory methods (T1–B).	3.3.5 3.3.8 1.2 2.5 2.7
• I selected spellings to reinforce sounds and letters that were covered during that session. These were given as homework to learn before the next session, to reinforce the letter combinations, as the lessons were 6 days apart. Some spellings were also from the History Curriculum shown in the long-term plans and some from Maths which he had difficulty with, in particular 'zero' because he mixed up Z with S (T1–D).	2.2 2.3
• I planned each session to follow the same sequence of tasks. This was to help him with his sequencing difficulties and to enable him to settle into the session quickly. The alphabet 'arc' was always first and I allowed up to 15 minutes for this task as I would remove letters and ask him to spot the missing letters and start the alphabet from M. He was awarded a merit stamp for successful completion.	2.5 2.9
• I gave a progress report to a colleague who covered the lesson in my absence together with a lesson plan. This was to enable her to work with the student on his continuing difficulty with the second half of the alphabet (T1–G).	3.3.6

5. Describe what happened when you carried out the work	Std
This student works best when he is in a quiet area and is separated from his peers. I settled him into the routine of the lessons by using the same sequence each time, constant praise and reward and encouragement to raise his self-esteem. He no longer resents the lessons and asks the teacher if 'today' is his special lesson.	1.2 2.9
The lessons were structured in easy steps and the instructions on the tape were clear and were repeated by myself regularly, stopping the tape to allow him plenty of time to memorise several instructions at once.	3.3.2 3.3.3
When a mistake occured I asked him to spot it himself and make a correction, this gave him the satisfaction of putting it right using his own judgement before moving on to the next step. This also increased his confidence of recognising mistakes and that mistakes can be corrected.	
The setting out of the foam letters to form an alphabet 'arc' is a kinaesthetic approach to memorising shape and sequencing of letters. I observed him and gave him an opportunity to spot any wrongly placed letters. If he failed to spot any error I would indicate the area but not the specific letter, he would then be able to spot the mistake himself, raising his confidence.	3.3.1 2.9 1.2
He stayed on task to complete the worksheets and I marked them during the session, giving written praise and a merit stamp from the school's Discipline 4 Learning policy (T1–E). This provided immediate recognition of achievement the correction reinforced leaving him a feeling of success. This in turn created a positive change in attitude and application to the work.	3.3.4
Spellings gave the student some difficulties, so I gave him spellings I knew he would be able to learn, to encourage him and I also introduced more difficult spellings to raise his expectations of achievement. As he disliked spelling because of his difficulty with it, I incorporated the learning of spelling into games available at school. This was to enable him to approach spelling in a less stressful attitude which in turn should help him learn more effectively as he enjoys the activity.	1.2 2.9

6. Describe any monitoring or assessment of the pupil you undertook	Std
I assessed the student's progress in the following ways:	
• By judging how well and quickly he set out the alphabet 'arc'. The assessment was made on the number of letters he misplaced and reversed. I used an assessment sheet I prepared using Microsoft Word to record each task in the lesson and I showed the sheet to teacher every 3–4 lessons.	3.2.2 2.4 3.2.3
• By observing him following the instructions to complete the worksheets and his competence in the handwriting and reading from previous lessons. I marked the worksheets with him and gave him an opportunity to correct any mistakes immediately to avoid any feelings of low self esteem.	3.2.3
• By giving a 5–6 word spelling test at the end of each session to establish if the combination of sounds were being recalled and used when spelling. If he was consistently getting a spelling wrong I would use other methods to teach spelling such as 'look, cover, write', foam letters and ghost writing on the table.	3.2.1 3.2.4 3.2.2 3.3.1
• I assisted in two Neale Analysis tests, one at the beginning of the Autumn term prior to the commencement of this activity and a second in the Summer term prior to his Annual Review.	3.2.1 3.2.4
• By administering a full spelling test for the end of year assessment for his Year Group. He sat his spelling test on a 1:1 basis to give him a more relaxed atmosphere to encourage successful results. I then analysed his scores against the word level objectives of the National Literacy Strategy (T1–J). This showed good phonic knowledge and word building despite his low score.	3.2.4 2.2 2.3
• By submitting a report to the SENCO on the student's progress and his change of attitude throughout the 'Beating Dyslexia' course. This report was submitted in full in the Annual Review distributed to all parties, including parents and outside agencies (T1H).	3.2.3 1.5

7. Evaluate your contribution to the activity, describing why it went well and what, if anything, you would do differently if you were repeating this work	Std
My contribution to this activity was to successfully plan and organise sufficient worksheets for each session and encourage the student to tackle new sounds and spellings with enthusiasm. He has outstanding success in completing the sequencing of the alphabet and the direction letters should face.	3.1.3
A misunderstanding between the letter S and Z was successfully redressed with no repeat errors and he learned to correctly spell his home village.	3.3.1
I would change the spelling homework by introducing a spelling book to be signed by his parents, as I felt he was practising the spellings at home.	3.1.4
As his reading age only improved slightly it may indicate that perhaps this programme was not extending him enough. After discussion with the SENCO it was decided to include a corrective reading scheme into the Individual Programme for this student.	3.2.2 1.5

Case study 2

Susan is a teaching assistant who works in an 11–16 high school. She mainly works in the mathematics department and ultimately hopes to be a teacher. Her Task 2 is included below.

Annex F2: Response sheet for task 2: Working with a small group

1. Your details

Name	
Your area(s) of expertise for this task	
School	
Name of teacher for this task	
Number of pupils for this task	

Where relevant in the following sections, the right-hand column is provided for you to record which Standards have been met.

2. Sources of evidence for this task

Document reference no.	Brief description	Std		
T2–A	Worksheets using Microsoft Word	2.4		
T2–B	Laminated mats using Microsoft Word	2.4		
T2–C	Lesson plan – signed by teacher	1.4		
T2–D	Worksheet showing modified approach	1.2		
T2–E	Lesson plan – modified approach	3.2.2		
T2–F	Constructive support and feedback to student	3.2.3		

3. Context
A brief, but anonymous, profile of the pupil with whom you have been working:

The group of students taking part in this activity were Year 7 students all working below Level 4 of the National Curriculum level descriptors and some are at the School Action stage on the SEN Code of Practice. They were withdrawn from the main Maths class to work on place value and subtraction by decomposition. The lessons and materials used were a practical project for an assignment I had to complete for the FDLT, Year 2, at UCN.

The group consisted of four girls and one boy all of whom I had assessed as having no understanding of place value while working with them during Maths lessons.

The nature of the activity:

The nature of the activity was a kinaesthetic approach to learning place value by using mats with columns and decimal coins. They then transferred each exchange on a worksheet, progressed to complete algorithms without the mats to finally demonstrating on the whiteboard the process of subtraction by decomposition.

4. Summarise how you contributed to planning the work, what you planned to do and why	Std
I made the resources used in this activity for an assignment as part of a FDLT course to explain and practice place value. The worksheets (T2–A) and mats were produced using Microsoft Word; then I laminated the mats to allow use of wipe-away pens (T2–B). Plastic decimal coins from the SEN resources were used as a visual aid to learning.	2.1 2.4 2.9 2.5 3.1.3
I discussed the planned work with the teacher and obtained his approval of the suitability of the worksheets (T2–C), then arranged which lessons to withdraw the students from. The teacher suggested resources from the 'Springboard Maths' folder available in school to provide extension worksheets, which I considered then chose 'Cracker Maths' from the SEN resources because they had puzzles to solve which I hoped would maintain the attention of the students.	1.4 3.1.3

5. Describe what happened when you carried out the work	Std
During the first two sessions when the activity was introduced, I arranged the room in a circle so all five students were facing each other in order to facilitate discussion as two students who were reticent and I encouraged them to ask questions and make suggestions	2.9 1.3 1.1
I read out the worksheets as a few of the students have reading difficulties and I wanted everyone to understand at the same pace, to avoid any feelings of individual failure. The students also completed, together, the set tasks of moving the coins on the mats.	1.2 2.1
I observed that one student completed all the tasks without difficulty, three were working steadily, discussing and helping each other, but one girl was having difficulties and trying to hide her worksheet with her arm, while copying the answers. She was therefore, not experiencing the kinaesthetic learning of moving the coins to understand the exchange involved (T2–D).	3.2.2 3.2.3
As this student has severe diabetes, she misses a lot of school and has concentration difficulties and has an IEP at the school action stage (T2–1). Her concentration dips during the maths lessons because it is before lunch. Therefore, taking this into account, I gave her 1:1 attention for part of the second session, asking her questions, encouraging her to move the coins, 'exchanging 10 of	2.5 2.8 1.2 3.2.2

these for 1 of those', giving her praise. She then moved into understanding the exchanging method and started to complete her worksheets herself, as the other students had done.

Using the 'Cracker Maths' worksheets because of my assessment from the previous lesson, would have not provided enough challenge (T2–E). The substitute activity was for each student to demonstrate on the whiteboard subtraction by decomposition of large numbers and these eventually progressed to the millions column to the amazement of the students. This was another example of kinaesthetic teaming which appears to meet their preferred learning style and greatly improved their self-esteem.	3.2.2 3.3.8 1.2 2.5

6. Describe any monitoring or assessment of pupils that you undertook	Std
I monitored the group as follows: • through observation of the students and assessing who asked the questions and who could provide the answers; • which student was able to help the most and thereby demonstrated more understanding; • how well each student could describe the process of exchanging between place value; • by marking their worksheets (T2–F) and giving feedback to students. I gave the teacher verbal feedback after each session of the progress and any difficulties the students had.	3.2.3 3.2.1 3.2.1

7. Evaluate your contribution to the activity, describing why it went well and what, if anything, you would do differently if you were repeating this work	Std
The set of lessons described here were successful and met the objectives of the students gaining an understanding of place value. The students demonstrated the concept of subtraction by decomposition with proficient knowledge. I was very pleased with my contribution to the progress of their maths but felt that the girl student who was having difficulty could benefit from further concrete learning to reinforce the process as her concentration levels wane.	3.3.5

Read through this draft and compare this draft to Paul's. In what ways do you think this draft is of a higher standard than Paul's?

When you plan your tasks you need to plan Tasks 1–3 at the same time. You will have the opportunity to discuss your drafts with your tutor from the training provider and hopefully a colleague from school. You need to start to identify the evidence you will provide. You will find that as you start to collect this evidence you may change your mind as to which are the best examples to develop as the contexts for Tasks 1–3. Some candidates decide to change during this drafting process and may be able to use the original example as a Task 4. The evidence can, as you would expect, be from a wide range and will include items such as planning sheets, notes, pupils' work, etc. It is important to identify your role in these items of evidence, e.g. your planning, your assessment of pupil. It is in your interest to show this clearly. Many candidates do this by highlighting the appropriate sections of the text.

Case study 3

Charlotte is a teaching assistant who has just been awarded HLTA status. She worked in schools for over 10 years and hopes to become a teacher in two or three years' time when she has completed an Honours Degree in Education. Her Task 3 is included as case study 3. Read this and compare it with the previous examples.

Annex F3: Response sheet for task 3: Working with a whole class
1. Your details

Name	
Your area(s) of expertise for this task	
School	
Name of teacher for this task	
Number of pupils for this task	

Where relevant in the following sections, the right-hand column is provided for you to record which Standards have been met.

2. Sources of evidence for this task

Document reference no.	Brief Description	Standard
T3/A(i)	Weekly Plans	2.2, 3.1.1
T3/A(ii)	Weekly Plans	3.1.1, 3.3.6
T3/A(iii)	Weekly Plans	3.1.1, 1.1
T3/B(i) & (ii)	Unit of Work	3.1.3
T3/B/(iii)	Witness Statement	1.4
T3/C(i) & (ii)	Lesson Plan	2.3, 3.1.2, 3.3.1, 2.4
T3/D	Lesson Plan	1.1
T3/E	Lesson Plan	2.5, 2.9
T3/F	Lesson Plan	3.2.2, 2.9
T3/G	Lesson Plan	3.2.1
T3/H	Lesson Plan	3.2.1
T3/I	Lesson Plan	1.6
T3/J	Lesson Plan	3.2.3, 1.6
T3/K	Example of Pupil's Work	3.3.5
T3/L	Example of Pupil's Work	3.3.5
	Teacher Verification	1.3, 3.3.4

3. Context *A brief, but anonymous, profile of the pupil with whom you have been working:*	Std
I carried out this task with the Year 2 class of 26 pupils. This class is a mixed ability class, all of whom had gained 2C or above in their recent literacy SATs (Standard Assessment Tests). Two children in the class have IEPs (Individual Education Plans), one as the child in question has been behind his peers since Year 1 (having missed much of his Reception year due to ill health) and one for behaviour, with targets focusing on following instructions and maintaining concentration. In addition to this, there are a further three pupils who are identified as needing extra support but they are not designated as having any specific learning difficulties. **The nature of the activity:** I undertook this task in order to further my experience of whole class planning, teaching and assessment. The task was carried out	

with the knowledge and approval of the Head Teacher and with the support of the class teacher.	
This task covered a week's literacy lessons, on teaching the children how to write a book review, but will focus on two of the four sessions I taught, in particular.	
The learning objectives (Doe T3/A(i)), which were linked to the NLS (National Literacy Stategy) Termly Objectives, were to write simple evaluations of books giving reasons (linked to the NILS writing objective T12) and to write in clear sentences using capital letters and full stops accurately (linked to NLS entence/word level work S5).	2.2

4. Summarise how you contributed to planning the work, what you planned to do and why	Std
The class teacher uses the Pelican Fiction writing resource which consists of units linked to the National Literacy Strategy and we usually use the unit plans provided as lesson plans with any necessary adaptation and differentiation for ability.	
The class teacher and I together looked at various ideas for the week's literacy lessons but settled on teaching the children how to write a book review. This part of the NLS had not been covered so far and I felt that it would be ideal as I am enthusiastic about books and I felt confident that I could teach these lessons on my own.	1.4 2.3
As all the children had gained a level 2C and above in their recent SATs I expected that the whole class would be able to join in the lesson without any additional support, other than that provided by me, or differentiation other than by the outcome of the written work that they would produce (Doc T3/A(iii)).	1.1
With this in mind I planned the week's literacy lessons, including plans for Tuesday (Doe T3/Ai(ii)) when I would be at college and the class teacher would be taking the lesson.	3.1.1 3.3.6
I took the suggested Pelican Fiction unit plans as a starting point for my lessons (Doe T3/B (i) & (ii)), However, immediately I felt that I needed to change the suggested text which was Little Red Riding Hood. I was aware that the children in this class had used this text on more than one occasion previously (in lessons on rhyming and time connectives) and I felt that the lessons would be more interesting for the children if I used a new text that they had not seen before. I checked with the class teacher that this would be appropiate (Doe T3/Bli(iii)), she confirmed it was a good idea	3.1.3 1.4 1.6

and helped me to select a Big Book which the children had not read as a class before. I wanted the text to have similar characteristics to Little Red Riding Hood, in that there was a rhythm to the text and that some repetition was involved and the class teacher, with her previous experience of the stories we had available, suggested Owl Babies by Martin Waddell.

I then took the two Pelican Fiction units and adapted them as I felt appropriate (Docs T3/C and T3/D). I needed to change the details and questions in the unit plans which referred to Little Red Riding Hood to make them appropriate to Owl Babies, writing my own new shared writing example and extending the questions on such things as the use of colour in the illustrations. I also wanted to include in my introduction a reminder of the different types of writing we had done as a class recently, in order to place the writing of a book review into context for the children

3.3.1
3.1.2

I also took out any parts of the unit plans which I felt were not appropriate. For example, while writing down what the children thought was the best part, the unit plans suggested that we could include a quote from the text. I felt that some of the children in the class would misconstrue this idea as permission to copy the text carte blanche from the book and that in a whole class situation it would take up a good deal of time to explain the idea behind quoting from books and could lead to confusion. I felt that this was a point which would be best left to a follow up session, when the children revisited writing a book review, which would then extend their skill in this.

The normal practice when adapting these Pelican Fiction unit plans is simply to write the adaptations and changes on a photocopy of the original. As I was to teach the whole class on my own, I wanted nothing to be left to chance and I decided to devise my own lesson plans (Docs T3/C and T3/D), in a similar format, but one that I felt I could follow easily, without the risk of missing anything out. I decided to word process the plans in order that I could colour code them more easily and effectively.

2.4

My learning objectives are in blue, my important teaching points are in red and my assessment opportunities are in green. This meant that when glancing down at the plans on my knees during the lesson I could see exactly which points were important and why.

I also included details on managing the children's behaviour during the lesson in order to maximise their learning and keep disruption to a minimum. These points I included in purple.

By devising a set of 'colour coded' plans I felt that should I lose sight of the lesson's objective or, if behaviour seemed to be going awry, I could quickly identify the thoughts and rationale I had had before the lesson in order to get the session back on track.

5. Describe what happened when you carried out the work	Std
No special point was made of telling the children why I was teaching the whole class. It is something that I have done on previous occasions and they are used to our normal classroom practice of the class teacher and I teaching half of the class each. However, I reminded the children that I expected the children to behave in the same way as they would normally when the class teacher was present and that I expected the same standards of behaviour.	1.3
During both sessions, I kept a close eye on where children sat on the carpet, moving any whose position I suspected would cause problems. This way disruptions were kept to a minimum and I could keep a close eye on any potential trouble. This is a behaviour management strategy employed by the class teacher and I thus ensured that my approach was consistent with hers.	3.3.4
Throughout both lessons, I kept a close eye on the children who need some extra support, making sure that they had understood what we had covered and asking them questions I felt sure that they knew the answer to, in order to increase their confidence and self-esteem. When I asked if anyone could remember what we called sub-headings one child, who sometimes needs support, remembered immediately. I knew that he had particularly liked my analogy (given in the previous week's lesson) about a submarine going under the sea (therefore sub-headings go under the main heading) and when he put his hand up I asked him to tell the rest of the class, which he did (T3/E)	1.1
The children appeared to enjoy these sessions but I felt that it was a long time for them to sit on the carpet (despite this being recommended in the Pelican Fiction unit plans). During the first session, the child who has an IEP for behaviour struggled to sit still for so long and in the end I had to move him and gently remind him that it wasn't just his own learning which he was interrupting but that of his classmates too. I made a note to ensure that he was more involved during the next session, by promising that he could give out the whiteboards etc., as he responds well to being given responsibility, which then usually improves his behaviour.	2.5 2.9

During the second session, I moved the lesson along at a quicker pace in order that the children spent less time on the carpet. I had planned for the children to work in pairs, using whiteboards, for the supported composition part of the lesson in order to maintain their concentration and interest. I had deliberately chosen certain pairings of children, for example boys who used this kind of exercise as an opportunity to chat to their friends were paired with girls who were keen to complete the task set. I also paired some of the lower attaining children with the highest attaining children in order that a mutually beneficial learning environment could be created. I wanted the less skilled children to benefit from the extra support and the more able children to experience having to think carefully about which knowledge and skills to transmit.	3.2.2 2.9

6. Describe any monitoring or assessment of pupils that you undertook	Std
After the lessons, I wrote my observations and assessments on my lesson plans (Docs T3), which is usual practice in the classroom in which I work. I do this in order to feedback to the teacher (and myself) how the lesson has gone, how individual children have done, what has worked, what needs improvement and any ideas for future planning.	3.2.1
I used observation and questioning as my main tools of assessment, using the plenary to ensure that the children had understood the main objectives of the lessons.	
I fed back to the class teacher my concerns about the length of time that the children were sitting on the carpet and she agreed that the suggested Pelican Fiction units plans were indeed too intense and when this 3.2.3 unit was taught next year, it may be better to spread it over a longer time She also suggested that possibly there were too many questions for them to answer and that this was something we could address next time.	3.2.3

7. Evaluate your contribution to the activity, describing why it went well and what, if anything, you would do differently if you were repeating this work	Std
Planning, teaching and assessing a week's literacy lessons has given me a greater insight into whole class teaching. The children certainly enjoyed writing book reviews and produced some good work.	3.3.5
I felt that the children had enjoyed the sessions but that there were improvements which could be made, should I teach these lessons again. I have recorded my evaluations of these lessons on the lesson plans for consideration next time in order that I may learn from them and improve my practice.	1.6
I learned that it is important to carefully monitor the time spent on the carpet, for example, if the children's learning is to be progressed effectively. The sessions were too intense, which led to some children finding it difficult to maintain concentration, especially on the more difficult questions. I have discovered, since teaching these sessions, that there is a set of Owl Baby figures available, which would open up the possibility of using them to create some kind of role play scenario, or maybe allowing me to incorporate drama into these lessons in the future. This would certainly alleviate the intensity of these sessions and allow the children to play a greater part in the lessons.	
One of the children also suggested that she thought she was like Sarah and I considered that it would have been interesting and fun then to develop this idea into a creative writing opportunity and ask the children to write about which owl they thought they were like and why. This could also be used as an extension activity for the higher attaining children, who finished their book reviews fairly quickly once we had settled down to write them.	
Next time I would like to write a book review of an appropriate book that I had read and enjoyed recently (and possibly arrange for my daughters to write one too of a book they had read) and share this with the children, demonstrating that I too was a reader, with likes and dislikes, just like them.	
It would also be interesting to incorporate ICT into these sessions in the future, encouraging children to use a word processor, possibly with the children working in pairs, interviewing each other and recording their answers, using a book review format, on a laptop.	2.4

> I am more confident as a result of teaching these sessions. It was gratifying to note that the children accepted me as their teacher without question, not even querying the situation when, at one point, their class teacher was at the back filing work into folders, a job they would normally see me do.

Case study 4

The final case study is that of Louise who decided to handwrite her Tasks 1–4. This is acceptable. A copy of a Task 4 is included.

Annex G4: Response sheet for task 4: Situation/event 4

Your details

Name
School

Where relevant in the following sections, the right-hand column is provided for you to record which standards have been met.

Sources of evidence for this task		
Document reference no.	**Brief description**	**Standard**
T/4/a	Risk assessment	3.1.4
T/4/b	Child protection form.	1.4
T/4/c	Policy Guidelines	2.7

Brief description of situation/event
A school trip with a Year 5 class. I was to support a child who had behaviour problems and needed 1:1 support.

Annex G4: Response sheet for task 4: Situation/event 4

Analysis: what you did, how and why, and with what consequences	Std
I met with the class teacher to go through the risk assessment for the trip. We also discussed the activities that would take part during the day and planned which group would start where (T4/4/a) one of the areas to visit was an archery demonstration. This was an area that can be a high risk area, because the child would be excited and if not dealt with correctly could trigger a problem with his behaviour. To ensure that this would not happen I explained that to go to that area he would have to walk not run and not to touch.	3.1.4
On the trip I was aware of where the child was at all times, but allowing, where possible, for him to have his space. As we walked around we talked about how the Tudors lived. The child started to tell me about issues that were happening at home. I listened. On return to school I went to see the school's child protection officer and told her what the child had said. I filled in the relevant forms (T4/4/b) and asked to monitor any changes in the child's behaviour and record anything else he told me.	1.4

Annex G4: Responses sheet for task 4: Situation/event 4

Learning points	Std
By being involved in the risk assessment and planning of the school trip I became familiar with different policies linked to school trips. For example the DfES guidance on 'Health and Safety of Pupils on Educational Visits' (T4/4/c).	2.7.

Index